Peace: RESTING IN GOD IN Every Storm

hope✳books collaborations

Published by hope*books

2217 Matthews Township Pkwy

Suite D302

Matthews, NC 28105

www.hopebooks.com

hope*books is a division of hope*media

Printed in the United States of America

hb
hope✶books

Table of Contents

Foreword

By Liz Caffman

Peace is one of the most sought-after things in the human heart. We long for it in our homes, our relationships, our minds, and our circumstances. Yet many people spend their lives chasing a version of peace that depends on everything around them being calm, predictable, and under control.

But life rarely works that way.

Storms come. Unexpected losses shake us. Uncertainty fills our minds. Difficult seasons arrive uninvited. In those moments, the peace the world offers quickly proves fragile—because it was never designed to withstand life's deepest storms.

The peace of God is different.

True peace is not simply the absence of trouble; it is the presence of God in the middle of it. It is a deep, settled confidence that even when the winds rage and the waves rise, we are still held securely in the hands of a faithful Father.

Scripture tells us that peace is one of the fruits of the Spirit—a work of God within us that cannot be manufactured by human effort. It grows as we learn to trust Him, surrender control, and allow His Spirit to shape our hearts. This peace does not always remove the storm, but it anchors us so that the storm does not remove our faith.

PEACE: Resting in God in Every Storm is a beautiful testimony to that truth.

Within these pages, you will encounter real stories from real lives—moments where fear, uncertainty, pain, and overwhelming circumstances could have easily taken control. Yet in the middle of those very situations, something extraordinary happened: the peace of God entered the story.

These testimonies remind us that God's peace is not theoretical. It is not just a verse we quote or a concept we admire. It is a living reality that meets us in hospital rooms, family struggles, seasons of grief, and moments of deep personal uncertainty. It is the quiet assurance that God is still present, still working, and still worthy of our trust.

Each story in this book stands as a witness to the fact that the peace of God is not reserved for perfect circumstances. It is available right in the middle of imperfect ones.

As you read, you may see reflections of your own journey within these pages. Perhaps you are currently walking through a storm of your own, wondering how to steady your heart when the winds feel strong. My prayer is that these stories will remind you that the same peace that carried others through their darkest moments is available to you as well.

God's peace does not promise a storm-free life. But it does promise that we never have to face the storm alone.

And when His Spirit fills our hearts, we discover something remarkable: even in the middle of the storm, we can rest.

About the Chapters

Chapter One

In this chapter, Vanessa King shares how God's unshakeable peace sustained her through the trials of military deployment, personal struggles, and high-stress environments. She recounts moments of danger and uncertainty, including rocket attacks in Afghanistan, where she experienced a profound sense of God's presence and protection. King emphasizes practical spiritual disciplines—meditating on God's attributes, abiding in His promises, and fixing one's eyes on Him—as tools to cultivate peace in the midst of life's storms. Ultimately, she encourages readers to trust God's faithfulness, lean on prayer and community, and allow His peace to guide and strengthen them through every challenge.

Chapter Two:

In this chapter, Rosalene Luxem reflects on finding God's peace amid the many wildernesses of her life, including chronic illness, abuse, and betrayal. She shares how, even in seasons of deep grief and heartbreak, God's covenant of peace remained steadfast, offering comfort, provision, and community support. Luxem emphasizes the importance of embracing pain rather than numbing it, learning to sit with sorrow while seeking the small, hidden springs of peace around us. Ultimately, she encourages readers to trust God's faithfulness, allowing His presence to sustain and restore them, even in the most desolate seasons of life.

Chapter Three:

In this chapter, Lauren Ulrich shares how she found God's peace while navigating the deep pain of fatherlessness. From childhood through young adulthood, she wrestled with the void left by an absent earthly father, experiencing anxiety, shame, and heartache, yet gradually learned to trust God as her faithful Heavenly Father. Through prayer, Scripture, and surrendering her brokenness to Him, she discovered that rooting her heart in God's promises allowed His peace to flourish in her life like a tree planted by a stream. Ulrich emphasizes that trusting God amid suffering brings enduring peace, healing, and the ability to flourish even in the midst of trials.

Chapter Four:

In this chapter, Dawn Fowler reflects on finding God's peace in the midst of life's chaos, grief, and uncertainty. She shares how walking with God taught her that peace is not dependent on circumstances but comes from a deep, trusting relationship with Him. Fowler emphasizes that surrendering worries, leaning into prayer, and embracing God's presence allows His peace to guide, comfort, and give clarity even during trials. Ultimately, she encourages readers to become "peace carriers," living in the midst of life's storms with God's love and light.

Chapter Five:

In this chapter, Karen Bedells shares how the peace of Jesus sustains us through life's chaos, hurt, and grief. Drawing from personal experiences—from childhood memories of worship to family losses and her nephew's illness—she illustrates that true peace is not temporary comfort but a lasting gift from God that transcends circumstances. Bedells emphasizes that peace comes through a personal relationship with Jesus, daily surrender, and reliance on His Word, allowing believers to rest and trust even in life's storms. Ultimately, she encourages readers to embrace His peace, to be complete in Him, and to share that peace with others.

Chapter Six:

In this chapter, Julie Baldwin explores how Jesus invites us to move from anxiety to lasting peace by trusting in God's provision and our value to Him. Drawing on her personal experiences with fear and worry, she illustrates how anxiety often stems from focusing inward and trying to control life, whereas Jesus calls us to shift our gaze outward toward His care. By seeking God's kingdom first, trusting His sovereignty, and embracing His non-anxious presence, we can cultivate a deep, enduring peace that influences not only our own lives but also those around us. Ultimately, Baldwin encourages readers to practice this trust daily, allowing God's peace to take root and transform their response to life's storms.

Chapter Seven:

In *Peace: Redeeming Our Wait*, Chere Wehling explores the difference between anxious, fear-driven waiting and a redeemed, Christ-centered waiting she calls *qāvâ*. Through personal stories—her daughter's hand injury and her husband's cancer diagnosis—she illustrates how trust in God transforms tense, anticipatory moments into opportunities for growth, healing, and intimacy with Him. Drawing on Scripture and Hebrew concepts like *gāal* (redemption) and *qāvâ* (waiting with hope and tension), she shows that peace comes not from control or solutions, but from leaning into God's presence daily. Ultimately, the chapter teaches that waiting well reshapes the heart, strengthens faith, and al-lows Jesus to provide "enough" for each moment.

Chapter Eight:

In this chapter, Becky Sims emphasizes the importance of listening for God's voice amidst the distractions and noise of everyday life. She shares personal stories, illustrating how God communicates with us—sometimes through immediate answers, other times through quiet nudges or the guidance of the Holy Spirit—and how prayer, Scripture, and reflection sharpen our ability to discern His direction. Sims encourages readers to walk in wisdom, trust God's timing, and remain continuously connected to Him, finding peace even in challenges. Ultimately, she shows that intentionally pausing to hear and follow God leads to greater faith, clarity, and confidence in our daily lives.

Chapter Nine:

In this chapter, Alana Deutschmann explores the spiritual and practical value of pursuing silence in a noisy world. She shares personal experiences showing how quieting external and internal distractions helps us become more present with God, ourselves, and others, allowing deeper awareness, reflection, and spiritual growth. Deutschmann distinguishes Christian silence from emptying the mind, emphasizing instead filling our hearts with Scripture, prayer, and attentiveness to God's presence. Ultimately, she encourages intentional practices—like mindful quiet, breath prayers, and reduced informational noise—as a pathway to cultivate peace, clarity, and authentic connection in daily life.

Chapter 1

Peace on the Battlefield: Experiencing God's Unshakeable Peace Amidst Trials

By Vanessa King

THE LORD BLESS YOU AND KEEP YOU; THE LORD MAKE HIS FACE SHINE UPON YOU, AND BE GRACIOUS TO YOU; THE LORD LIFT UP HIS COUNTENANCE UPON YOU, AND GIVE YOU PEACE.
NUMBERS 6: 24-26, NKJV

In my early 20s, I was a newly commissioned Air Force Officer engaged to be married, but those carefully laid plans were slipping through my fingers. I distinctly remember feeling panic rise within me as the weight of the news that I would be deployed on what was supposed to be our wedding date settled on my shoulders. Tears were threatening to spill over, but I could not cry at that point because I was participating in a training exercise at a different duty station and had zero places to run and hide the sob that was choking me.

I managed to keep it together and, at the first opportunity, I called my fiancé to break the news. He handled the news with more grace than I had. God used his calm demeanor to steady me. With his clarity of mind, he suggested we call our parents to see what they might think. After discussing the change of plans, and through the incredible will of God, we were able to work out a solution.

Through that unexpected detour, my husband and I were actually able to get married earlier in an intimate ceremony and still have our "normal" wedding on our regularly scheduled date. Both were delightful experiences as we got to celebrate with loved ones from near and far. All of this was made possible by a loving God who works in ways we cannot even begin to fathom, but they are always for our good and His glory.

Less than a week after our "normal" wedding, I deployed to Afghanistan, loaded down with my gear, a Kindle Paperwhite, and some homemade cookies.

I was a 24-year-old, newly married Air Force officer, struggling with my identity as a woman in the military and as a child of God. If I were honest with myself, I wanted to be a wife and a mother, but the world around me bombarded me with the message that "that wasn't enough". My deepest desire was to take care of my home and eventually homeschool my children. My internal struggle vacillated between my pride of wanting to "wow" someone when I told them about my military career versus being "just" a wife and a mother. I wanted to please the world with my choices instead of listening to the prodding of the Holy Spirit and His leading.

The journey to Afghanistan was circuitous, with a few stops and several nights in Kazakhstan along the way. When I arrived, my mind was sluggish from jet lag and hunger. Amid the whirlwind of paperwork, being issued my IBA (Body Armor) and weapon, and driving on pothole-infested roads, my boss filled me in on what was happening.

He warned me that insurgent activity was heavy, and we would have to hit the deck when the "incoming" warning blared over the intercom.

This would prove to be true. Nearly every night, we had to either shelter in place or run to the nearest bunkers for safety. For the duration of my deployment, all rocket attacks occurred during my shift, the night shift.

There was one particular night when the rocket attacks were constant. We stayed in the bunkers for a long stretch of time. Eventually, there was a lull in the action, so we slowly began to emerge and return to work on the flight line. No sooner had we settled back into our work rhythm than a volley of rockets made their way toward us.

I didn't have enough time to make it to a bunker. The "incoming" alarm did not send out its warning before the rockets arched through the inky black sky. I hit the ground, my left cheek pressed against the warm asphalt. I glanced up, watching the rockets come over like shooting stars of death.

At that moment, I thought I was going to die. In that shadow of death, it seemed as if time stood still and all became quiet. I was not filled with fear. I felt a peace that to this day I still cannot fully explain. It felt as though I was transported to another place where there was no more anxiety or panic, no more fear or agony. I was acutely aware of the presence of the Holy Spirit overshadowing me. I know it was because of God answering the many prayers of His people, lifting up petitions to our Heavenly Father for protection.

It was a peace that surpasses all understanding and comfort that comes only from God. Even though I thought I was staring down death, I was ready for whatever the Lord willed and sought His face in the midst of the darkness.

I thought of my husband back home in our little apartment, and I prayed that the Lord would shower him with love and care and surround him with the peace that I was experiencing. As I waited for the rockets' impact, it felt as though my heart was as light as a feather, even though I did not know if I was going to survive.

Seconds later, a rocket made an impact several yards away. The ground shook as one, two, three more collided around the flight line, shrapnel ricocheting everywhere.

Lying there, the ground shaking beneath me, not knowing if any moment would be my last, I continued to feel His presence with me. It was palpable and comforting. I'll never forget it.

Our office had a large map of the airfield, where we would mark the rocket impacts with a pin. We were astonished that none of the rockets managed to hit any of our aircraft despite how close the rockets were to us. It was as if an angel was swatting them away.

It was a miracle no one was injured or killed that night. I knew that the prayers of God's people were putting a hedge of protection around us, and His Spirit granted me that peace. That moment was pivotal in reminding me that I am a daughter of God—beloved and cared for, even when it felt like the Lord might be calling me home.

I am sure I am not the only one who struggles to abide in the peace and comfort from the Lord, especially in the daily rhythms of our lives. I trust that the Lord, in His wisdom, provides ample opportunities for us to experience His peace on this side of heaven.

I am growing in my trust in the wisdom of the Lord as I continue to walk with Him. Through much prayer, fumbling, and humbling, I have realized that fixing my eyes on Jesus, the author and perfecter of my faith, continually refines and sanctifies me.

Here are several different spiritual disciplines that I've implemented in my own life that have helped me grow in peace from the Lord. The first point was introduced to me through a dear friend and mentor who encouraged me to practice it, especially when life was anything but peaceful. Others were revealed to me through God's grace and the power of the Holy Spirit working in my own life. You will find that they are not exercised in isolation but often flow seamlessly from one to another.

1.   Meditate on the attributes of God.

2.   Abide in the promises of God.

3.   Fix your eyes on God.

There are endless scenarios in life where peace can feel impossible to attain.

Maybe...

You're enduring the loss of a loved one, someone you can not imagine living life without, and the ache in your heart is impossible to articulate, so sobs and crying out to the Lord are all you can do to help ease the heartache.

You are struggling with how to navigate a relationship that brings you constant grief and pain. Maybe the individual is sarcastic in a cutting way or antagonistic towards you, making it impossible to communicate effectively. Maybe it is what that person is *not* doing that causes the most pain.

You are in the trenches of motherhood and cannot imagine a day when the kids will be able to feed themselves or finally start sleeping through the night. You keep thinking to yourself, "When they start XYZ, then I can finally breathe." The nights are long, the days are short, and you are dreading nighttime or being left alone.

The deepest desire of your heart is unfulfilled, no matter how many times you pray and long for it to happen. It is a godly desire, one that would be honoring to the Lord, and you can not understand why it would be withheld from you.

You are in a crushing work environment where the stress threatens to cripple you each day you step through the door. Your boss is unsupportive, and you long for the day when you can move on to something else, but you have no idea when that day will come.

Or you're on the battlefield where there are rocket attacks every night, and you do not know if you're going to make it out alive.

I have experienced all of these scenarios. I can look back and see how the Lord tenderly cared for me in those chapters of my life. There are experiences when I felt the presence of the Lord acutely and others when I felt alone, even though I knew intellectually that my God was there with me.

It was not until recent years that I have been able to distill tangible ways I can exercise my faith in scenarios that are challenging and stretching. Each one continues to sanctify and refine me as a child of God.

Meditate on the attributes of God

During one particularly hard season, a dear friend and mentor took the time to listen to my anguish as I sought to understand and untangle everything I was experiencing and had experienced in the past. I no longer focused on the beauty and glory of who God is. I needed to have my heart and mind rebuilt on truth and not the lies that I was listening to and telling myself.

What she encouraged me to do would change my walk with the Lord forever. She encouraged me to meditate on the attributes of God. This singular faith-building activity has carried me through many dark nights and days and has helped me to seek the face of God amidst my circumstances.

I am paraphrasing her lesson to me here:

"When you find yourself starting to spiral, say out loud (if possible), 'Stop,' or wear an elastic hair band around your wrist and snap it against your skin. This will help to break you out of whatever spiral you might find yourself in. Then start at the letter A, and think of an attribute of God that begins with 'A.' Awesome. God is awesome! Move on to 'B,' for Beautiful. God is beautiful! 'C' is for Comforter. God is my comforter! Keep going until you run out of ideas. Then start back at the beginning. You can also list as many attributes as you can, starting with a certain letter, and see how far you can go."

When I practice this, I find that I am taking my eyes off of me and the swirling mess around me, and fixing my eyes on Jesus. Inevitably, my heart stops racing, and I can focus on the Truth, Beauty, and Goodness of God.

Abide in the promises of God

Focusing on the attributes of God naturally flows into meditating on the promises of God. While meditating on those attributes, you start to settle into Who God is. God is infinite, so it is impossible for our finite brains to comprehend everything about Him.

With this in mind, we can shift our meditation or add our meditations onto the promises of God.

There are so many promises of God we find in the Bible that it may feel overwhelming to pick just a few. To start, I encourage you to spend time in God's Word and/or find a devotional that can help you. Pick one to three promises to memorize and absorb. Once you have tucked these away in your heart, you can pick a few more to add to your treasures.

Three promises that I cling to in times of trial are:

"Let us hold fast the confession of *our* hope without wavering, for He who promised *is* faithful."

Hebrews 10:23, NKJV

"And the Lord, He *is* the One who goes before you. He will be with you, He will not leave you nor forsake you; do not fear nor be dismayed."

Deuteronomy 31:8, NKJV

"You will keep *him* in perfect peace, *Whose* mind *is* stayed *on You*, because he trusts in You."

Isaiah 26:3, NKJV

Reflecting on these promises will help reinforce the attributes of God that you were meditating on earlier. Tucking these away in your heart will be helpful when you need something to readily minister to your soul in your time of need.

There are occasions when I struggle with anxiety when my husband travels for work. If I'm not careful, I can allow these thoughts to start going through a spiral of worst-case scenarios.

I am grateful that with the help of the Holy Spirit, these moments are becoming easier to recognize, so I can start reminding myself of these promises about God's character and snap myself out of the spiral that looms ahead. I take a moment to pray and breathe and say to myself, aloud if the opportunity allows, Isaiah 26:3.

You might even find yourself drawing from the wellspring of truth for days, weeks, and months. Trials are bound to come, so cultivate the Truth of the gospel and mine the depths of Peace.

Fix your eyes on God

The natural progression from meditating on the attributes of God and abiding in the promises of God is fixing your eyes on God.

You might not be conscious of it, but now that you've taken the time to saturate your mind and heart with the truth, fighting back the lies that threaten your peace, you have been fixing your eyes on God and not your circumstances.

I encourage you to pray for peace throughout these disciplines. Coming before the throne of grace provides you with the opportunity to lay your burdens at our Heavenly Father's feet.

Ask the Holy Spirit for help in keeping your focus on Christ and not on your own circumstances. We can get caught up in whatever the moment brings. With practice, we can start to understand how our trials and temptations point us to Christ and rely on Him for strength and peace.

We live in an easily distracted world. In order to cultivate time to spend meditating on these things, I encourage you to silence your phone or put it in another room. Be intentional with your time with the Lord. Set aside time during your morning commute to pray instead of listening to the radio or a podcast. Wake up a little earlier or do it right before bed.

Bonus Tip: As I have reflected on the experiences that stand out boldly in my walk with the Lord, those that have sanctified and matured me by God's grace, I know that the prayers of God's people were instrumental in all of those situations. If you find yourself walking through a valley, I encourage you to reach out to trusted friends and family and ask them to pray fervently for you. We should share our burdens and petition our Holy God together.

Peace is something that can be cultivated through prayer, time in the Word, and petitioning the prayers of trusted family and friends.

Some time ago, I was struggling with a difficult relationship. It was a professional relationship that added a layer of complexity to an already stressful situation. I couldn't hand in my two-week notice and find a new job because of the kind of work I was in. I was stuck, and I dreaded going to bed every night knowing the type of work environment that I had to face the next day.

I hadn't learned the spiritual discipline of going through the Attributes of God at this time, but I did spend much time in prayer, time in God's Word, and petitioning the prayers of trusted family and friends. My church family was the hands and feet of Christ during this time. Through these means, I started to focus more on Christ, praying for a softened heart that wouldn't grow bitter and remind myself that my identity was in Christ, not what this individual was projecting onto me. Over the course of time, I was able to face the challenges of each day with more grace, peace, and fortitude than I had before.

Utilizing these spiritual exercises of meditating on the attributes of God, abiding in the promises of God, and fixing your eyes on God will continue to cultivate the wellspring of peace in your life even when the storm rages on.

You will be equipped with tools that point you to Christ and not to your own circumstances.

I offer you Moses' priestly blessing, "The LORD bless you and keep you; the Lord make his face shine upon you, and be gracious to you; The Lᴏʀᴅ lift up His countenance upon you, And give you peace" (Numbers 6: 24-26; NKJV).

Here are some more beneficial tools that can further enrich your walk with the Lord.

Memorize scripture: Write on an index card the verses you would like to memorize and meditate upon, and stick them in your Bible. Do not memorize *just* to memorize, but meditate on them.

Keep a prayer &/or thankfulness journal: Having a prayer &/or thankfulness journal will be a treasure for you and will leave a legacy for your loved ones to read if you want them to. They will get to see firsthand how our Heavenly Father answered your prayers. A prayer &/or thankfulness journal helps us pull away from our self-centered desires and forces us to take stock of all that we have been blessed with already. There is always something to be thankful for this side of heaven!

Not too long ago, I was really struggling with contentment. Intellectually, my mind was aware that all of my needs were met, I was blessed with a wonderful family, and the health concerns that were troubling me were much better after getting them addressed. However, my heart felt dull towards life. I couldn't understand why I was so disgruntled.

As I was washing the dishes one day, I realized I hadn't been reading my Bible. My time with God became rote. We prayed as a family before meals, before we started our homeschool day at the table, and before bed. We attended church on Sunday and had family worship every night. Why did I feel so dry spiritually?

I was not spending time with my Lord and my God. My eyes were open to the reality that because my circumstances were so good, I was relying on myself to get through the day. I wasn't spending time in His Word or praying. I had completely neglected strengthening this muscle of reflecting on the riches of His character.

I dusted off my prayer and gratitude journal and started to keep track of them again. I was compelled to read through my past prayer requests and answers to prayer and was so encouraged by the faithfulness of God and hard providences that He sanctified me through. It was a blessing to remember how His hand worked in the lives of my family and friends.

I was grateful that the Holy Spirit pricked my dull heart to cultivate intentional time with Him. I asked a friend to pray that I would continue to be faithful in my daily time with the Lord and not see it as a bland experience, but one that is life-giving. I am so prone to forget the Peace that God brings to His people.

I hope these tools bless you and encourage you in your walk with the Lord!

May God bless you richly and may you feel His peace!

Chapter 2

Springs in the Wilderness: Finding Peace in Pain

By Rosalene Luxem

For your Maker is your bridegroom,
   his name, God-of-the-Angel-Armies!
Your Redeemer is The Holy of Israel,
   known as God of the whole earth.
You were like an abandoned wife, devastated with
   grief, and God welcomed you back,
Like a woman married young
   and then left," says your God...
"For even if the mountains walk away
   and the hills fall to pieces,
My love won't walk away from you,
   My covenant commitment of peace won't fall apart."
The God who has compassion on you says so.

Isaiah 54:5,6,10, MSG

This is not my first time in the wilderness. It is not unfamiliar; the terrain has become a sort of home, and wandering deeper into the barrenness is a call I know well. I find myself driven to the desert by the choices and actions of others and circumstances outside of my control.

Will El Roí—the God who sees me—meet me here in compassion and provision? Will He once again, as He's done before, open my eyes to the springs around me and lead me to places of quiet rest?

My first wilderness was disease. My teenage and young adult years were spent mostly in bed, suffering from countless symptoms of chronic Lyme Disease. Years seemingly wasted as I fitfully slept between writhing pain, heavy anxiety, and hundreds of pills a day.

Peace found me often in the companionship and faithfulness of my family, taking care of me and sitting in the silence with me, my best friend coming by after work to hold my hand, and my dog lying with me on the couch. Always, it was simple and small things that brought comfort and light and held me through the darkest days. Pain was always there, yet peace became more real than I'd ever known. I was desperate for it, and I learned to seek it out in the quiet chaos of long-term illness. As I sought, I always found. I learned that God is not a withholding Father, and He became bigger and nearer than even my disease.

The landscape would soon shift, leading me into my second wilderness: abuse. I married my first husband at just 20 years old, and the deserts of disease and abuse intertwined. I thought no one else could want me, so when I was shown slight care and attention, I committed to a marriage with someone who consistently hurt me.

Early in the relationship, cutting remarks began about my appearance, my personality, and my identity. I began to feel insecure and undesirable, but at least I was being chosen...somewhat. Cutting remarks turned into manipulation, and manipulation turned into force, and then over and over the confusing cycle went of verbal and emotional abuse, love-bombing (excessive and overwhelming affection used as a manipulation tactic), my body being taken advantage of, and then anger and shame that somehow I was the one to blame for unwanted sexual behaviors.

My marriage was a mess just a few months in. I was scared of being hurt and scared of leaving my husband alone, in case he'd choose unfaithfulness. I became a babysitter. I was ashamed of my body and the way it couldn't be and do what he wanted. I was scared of being hurt over and over, so I tried to do anything and everything to make him happy. I couldn't be away from him without getting punished for it in some form, so I became isolated.

We had a baby together just a few weeks after my 22nd birthday. My pregnancy was spent mostly alone in an apartment with almost no furniture. I felt heavy and depressed, with a pit in my stomach and the thought that I was even more undesirable now. Even in carrying his child, my body was somehow wrong and bad. I was lonely and scared, and I thought all of this must be my fault. *Maybe I made bad choices. Maybe I brought us to isolation. Maybe I chose this. Maybe we really couldn't afford furniture, and it was my fault that I didn't have a couch to sit on or a table to eat at.*

When my son was only a little over a year old, I'd had enough. The desire for other women, addiction to pornography, and violent sexual aggression towards me had become unbearable, and though my anxiety was at an all-time high at the thought of being alone and the path forward after speaking out about the abuse, I knew if I stayed, I'd end up dead eventually. So I took my baby, and I ran. I went to my friends, my family, the church, the police, and the legal system. I spent years fighting for justice for myself and my son, and spent years being wrung dry by the systems and people that were meant to protect us.

This was a season of heavy loss, punctuated by the loss of friends and our church home, which was unable to accept the painful situation we were in, so they dismissed us. I experienced tremendous loss of my own innocence, ripped away by abuse and a legal system that perpetuated the cycle, bargaining away criminal offenses on the grounds of marriage. I've never felt more humiliated, as if I were a dog whose owner could do with me as he pleased. When I begged for justice and for someone to see, I was cut down even more.

In this wilderness, Jesus brought peace in the most beautiful ways. El Roí saw us, and in seeing, saw to it that we would be provided for in every sense. We were shown care by a ragtag bunch of friends. They came unexpectedly and rallied around my son and me, willing to be with us in our brokenness. We had a sweet and safe home of our own. I owned a thriving business. I was living in miraculous health and wholeness in my body, able to be a single mom with all that entails. I also walked through years of court. Peace came in quiet nights. I cried before the Lord about why I was here, wondering if it would ever end and if there would ever be true justice.

Here in this place of pain and peace, I found Jesus to be the most constant. Just as He met me in the wilderness of disease, He met me in the wilderness of abuse. And He called me by name and said I am His, and He dusted me off and held my hand, and I learned that my Maker is my Husband and He is a good Husband.

As I healed, I discovered I could trust again, and I prayed and therapied my way into a second marriage with a man I truly loved and believed was *good*. Finally, a man we could trust. Finally, a partner to raise my son with. And so, at just under 27, I got remarried in a beautiful and redemptive backyard ceremony at my parents' home. Our closest family and friends came to bless what God had brought about and entrust my son and me into the hands and heart of my new husband. We could all breathe now. The worst was over, and I was being invited out of the wilderness.

For a time, it really was a dream. Not a "nothing is ever wrong" kind of dream, but a redemptive, healing, sweet time. We were building a beautiful life together, and he was my best friend and a safe landing for my son and me.

I find myself now freshly led into my third wilderness. At the very end of 2025, I discovered that my second husband had been living a life of unfaithfulness. Out tumbled years of near-constant deceit; the man I loved had been leading another life I didn't know about, filled with consistent betrayal, actively online as if he were a single man dating many women, lying about his name, his age, and everything else under the sun. And then he was caught, and it all fell apart. He was supposed to be the good one. This was supposed to be redemption and restoration, and last the rest of my life.

So here I am in the wilderness of heartbreak and betrayal. My heart is heavy, and my body is worn out in the wake of uncovering the lies. Twice now, my marriage has ended because of the unfaithfulness of men who were supposed to love and protect, and instead turned their swords of harm towards my son and me. I really thought I could trust this one.

Again, I find myself staring down disappointment, betrayal, and crushed dreams. Again, I lay awake at night wondering how this has happened. And again, I find myself in the loving care of Jesus. Again, I am broken, and again I will be bandaged up and made whole. Again, I see His hand of grace and deliverance, preparing and guiding and holding us.

I've been here before, and I know where to run to find peace. This peace is not the absence of my sorrow, my troubles, or my pain. This peace is my underlying source, flowing as I wrestle with reality. Holding, wrapping, renewing, reviving, and standing me right back up in the light of Him who Himself is peace.

In all of the wildernesses I've lived in, there has been an invitation to welcome into my heart the pain and grief of it all. Wouldn't it be easier to numb? Wouldn't it be easier to deny? But as I've opened myself up and taken the hand of pain and looked it in the eyes and said "Yes, I see you", peace has come just as swiftly to grasp my other hand and bear me up in her arms when I can't go any further. Peace has softened the presence of pain. Pain has not left, and I've lived enough in my short 31 years to know it is not going anywhere. And thank goodness, neither is peace.

Embracing the Wilderness

As humans, I think we naturally wish we could bypass the wildernesses of life. We can be tempted to view them as only a transitional place, thinking that if we can just get through it, things will be good again and life will be back on track. Wouldn't it be lovely if we could always live in the peaceful, green pastures? Pain and sorrow are not pleasant, and sometimes the invitation to meet God in the wilderness feels more like a forced exile than anything else. And while it is valid and aligned with God's original design for perfection that we don't want to live in hardship, I have also found that when I accept the grief of losing and surrendering my own desires of what I thought my life would look like, and when I embrace the truth that God is here in all of my suffering, the wilderness terrain evens out a bit before me. Though the ground is still dry and cracking and sandy, making my feet tired and my soul weary, I am not alone. There is room to acknowledge the hard reality while also seeking out the goodness and life still present here.

I am learning more every day that embracing the wilderness does not look like plastering on a smile, pulling myself up by my bootstraps, or just muscling through. That will only bring more exhaustion and pain as the grief compounds, unattended. Embracing the wilderness looks like allowing my pain to be felt and seen and heard, and it is not easy or pretty or quick. It is not a one-and-done kind of feeling the pain. It is an over and over again, every morning when I wake up with grief heavy in my chest, choosing not to shove it aside. It demands my time and attention, interrupting me throughout my days, when out of nowhere the tears start falling, and my body breaks down, and all I can do is curl up on the floor for a few minutes. It looks like a journal page, so tear-stained it is unreadable. It looks like ugly-crying in front of others, even though I so badly wish I could just hold it together and convince myself and everyone around me that it's all just fine.

It takes hard, intentional work to settle into the season we are in and acknowledge that life is still lived here, even when it's desolate. Yet in my years of holding heaviness, I have never regretted any of the time spent sitting with my sorrow. And I think that's because I have gleaned the fruit of past wilderness seasons, and I understand that before the Lord, this is holy work. This is not a waste of His time, so it is not a waste of mine. I do not belong to a God who wants me to produce and perform endlessly, who is tapping His watch impatiently, wishing I would just get over my problems and heal already. I belong to a compassionate God. A wrap-you-up-in-a-blanket-and-bring-you-tea kind of Father. A man of sorrows, well-aquainted with grief. A nurturing Mother, broken-hearted over Her children's suffering and ready to hold me for as long as I need.

This embrace of the wilderness is not a linear process or a task of just trying to feel it so you can get past it and move on, but it is a lifelong practice of learning to let pain in even though it's uncomfortable, and having the grace and patience that allow sorrow to be held with care and tenderness. This opening up to pain softens the heart to be able to receive straight from the hand of God. It has been in my deepest and darkest nights that I've felt the most held and experienced the supernatural nearness of the Lord, bringing peace and comfort where nothing and no one else can. Oh, it is beautiful when we learn this and can live into it. It is like finding a spring in this dry land that is just dripping with mercy.

Finding Peace in Pain

As I reflect on my history with Jesus and the many paths we've walked, I can confidently say that I have never known a day without His peace. And I have had a lot of bad days. In fact, sometimes I think to myself that, to the outside world, I must look like a very unlucky woman, dealt a heavy hand of suffering with a few good days scattered here and there. But when I think back on my life, I see a beautiful, beautiful story. One that tells of the nearness and faithfulness of Jehovah Shalom—the Lord is Peace—holding me through everything.

I find strength as I reflect on God's faithfulness, and when I choose to run with my son into the arms of the One who will never fail, even when husbands and fathers do. I experience rest as I look around and see the ways He has already worked to surround us with beauty and community. Holy Spirit peace binds me up and starts its healing process in the car as I cry with my mother, and she prays over me, in my father's protective presence, out mowing my lawn, and in my grandfather's voice calling to say he will stand by me and speak up for justice. Women gather around—sisters, cousins, friends, mothers, grandmothers—all here to hold my pain and do my dishes and make my bed and hang my shelves. Peace is waiting even in the heaviness of holding my big, half-grown-up son as we grieve and remember and ask Jesus to be near.

Spirit-given peace is not mustered up by human will; it is not grand and imposing, replacing every other thought and feeling or pushing aside reality. It is often small and sort of hidden, and sometimes calls for a bit of creativity to be sought out and noticed, but it is always accessible.

When you are walking the lonely and painful path of the desert, there are simple invitations to rest all around. Perhaps the sun is breaking through the fog and peace is waiting to be soaked up in the quiet moments spent each morning brewing a cup of coffee, in your drives to school drop-off as you listen to your kids' expectant chatter, in the comforting normalcy of a workday or errand-running or dish-washing, and even in the tears that you wish would stop filling your eyes. Peace can be found alone as you sit with your sorrow and in the company of unexpected laughter shared with friends, in the secluded late-night hours spent pouring your heart into your journal, and in the full sanctuary on a Sunday morning. All around, new mercies are ready to be leaned into.

Creating new rituals and routines that make room for rest can feel nearly impossible when we are in the throes of grief, but I have found that starting with small acts of caring for ourselves is a gentle and gracious way to experience peace in the midst of pain. This could be something as simple as a few minutes set aside in the morning to read a Psalm or pray a liturgy, a quick afternoon walk full of deep breaths, or a cup of tea at bedtime. Maybe it's committing one day a week to being extra kind to yourself by eating your favorite meal, creating a piece of art, or spending time with those you feel the most loved by. Even in the hard things, life is lived, and peace is present, and goodness is available for you.

Resting in God's Peace

While all of the above is true — that embracing our wilderness and acknowledging our pain is an invitation to peace, and peace is always accessible — it is also true that sometimes deep breathing feels impossible, and sometimes I forget to breathe at all. Even still, the promises of God remain. Unshakable in all His ways, faithful to keep His word, this is the God who is the peace I need.

Some days we are walking in the wilderness, moving on through, and some days we are just lying down on the hot sand, too tired to go on, while He shields us from the sun. Some days we are skipping along with pain just barely at our heels and peace as a crown on our head, and other days pain seems to have sat down right on top of us while peace sits nearby, but not quite close enough to touch. May we learn that no matter where we find ourselves, we can rest in the compassionate and covenant-keeping God, who calls us who are deserted and broken-hearted:

> ...For even if the mountains walk away
> > and the hills fall to pieces,
> My love won't walk away from you,
> > my covenant commitment of peace won't fall apart."
> The God who has compassion on you says so.
> > > Isaiah 54:9-10, MSG

I know this to be so true. I know the love and peace of God to be consistent and reliable. I know that when life shatters and people fail, when sorrow and brokenness seem to overshadow all else, God's love doesn't walk away from me. He doesn't break His covenant of peace with me. And He doesn't break it with you, either.

God is good, and He is trustworthy, and His love and peace are promised even when everything else has been destroyed or stolen or you find yourself in a desert you didn't plan to walk through or were sent to by someone or something else. Isn't that just the mercy of God, to keep His word in the face of the broken promises and covenants around us? This is why I can rest in Him: because I know it with my whole body, because I've lived it before, and I know there are springs all around in the desert.

I don't know where my journey leads next. I am fresh into this new season of heartbreak, and it's all looking pretty barren. But in all that emptiness, I see a vast space where I'm sure something is going to spring up. Having been through sickness, abuse, betrayal, and loss of all kinds, I know the path ahead is not easy or short. I know healing is slow, and progress will be hard to see in the moment. And I know I'm going to be met with invitations to experience peace at every turn, because I have seen the way our good Father does not leave us alone on the path of pain; He always makes a way for beauty, redemption, and restoration to spring up, because it is simply His nature to do so in keeping His covenant with us.

My prayer for both you and me, dear reader, is that as we reflect on our lives and ask for divine perspective to see where the Lord has kept His covenant of peace with us, we feel the truth deep in our spirits that He will be faithful again, just like He has been faithful before. That one day we will look back and see even more clearly the goodness and grace of Jesus. I pray that wherever you find yourself right now, and however long you've been here or will be here, you can open your hands to what God has for you, even if that means opening them to some sorrow. When you open those clenched hands, may peace be quick to fall into them, and your heart quick to hang onto it.

Next Steps

As we lean into pain and allow it to be felt, it is equally important to lean in and allow peace to be felt beside it. Take some time today to journal about this. Is there a wilderness you are being asked to embrace? Can you identify threads of peace and goodness, even here, no matter how small? How do you best find rest? Can you make space to enter into God's rest and let His covenant of peace hold you?

A Blessing for Peace in the Wilderness

Blessed are we who are living in the wilderness.
Who have arrived here not because we sought it out,
Or because we wandered away from You,
But because brokenness abounds, and we are impacted by it.

Blessed are we who are brave in the wilderness,
Because we know You are with us.
We take the hand of pain and allow it to come close.
We walk beside suffering, even though it is not the friend we asked for.
May peace come swiftly.
Blessed are we, even here, even now,

For You give peace in the wilderness;
Peace for our broken, heavy hearts.
Peace for our tired and aching feet.
Peace for our eyes, that sometimes can't stop crying,
And sometimes have no tears left to shed.
Peace for our hopes, hanging on by a thread.

And blessed are You, Jesus,
Our covenant-keeping Prince of Peace,
Who gently leads and guards,
Who tenderly comforts and holds,
Who causes springs to come forth in every wilderness,
Until at last we can dwell in the green pastures of eternity.

Amen

Chapter 3

Rooted in the Father's Love: Finding His Peace in Your Pain

By Lauren Ulrich

BUT BLESSED IS THE ONE WHO TRUSTS IN THE LORD, WHOSE CONFIDENCE IS IN HIM. THEY WILL BE LIKE A TREE PLANTED BY THE WATER THAT SENDS OUT ITS ROOTS BY THE STREAM. IT DOES NOT FEAR WHEN HEAT COMES; ITS LEAVES ARE ALWAYS GREEN. IT HAS NO WORRIES IN A YEAR OF DROUGHT AND NEVER FAILS TO BEAR FRUIT.

JEREMIAH 17:7-8, NIV

I was born with a hole in my heart. It was an early morning in August, over 40 years ago. After a whirlwind of a delivery, the doctor discovered a heart murmur in my tiny, delicate chest. A hole had formed in my heart to cause abnormal blood flow. I was put under the watchful care of a pediatric cardiologist and in the warmth of an incubator over the next few weeks. Fortunately, I grew to be a healthy, full-term baby, and the hole in my heart eventually closed.

However, another invisible hole in my heart remained as I grew to be a young girl. I'll never forget the first time I consciously felt this undeniable void and heartache.

I was in preschool. I had been asked to draw a picture of my family on construction paper with crayons. First, I cheerfully enjoyed making stick-like figures of my mom and myself with our dog and a sun shining above us. I admired my picture until I began glancing around at my classmates' drawings, noticing one after another included a tall dad in their family. Suddenly, my family felt so small, so different, and so incomplete. And I wanted to hide my picture. I wanted a different family and a different story than the one I found myself in at that tender age of four. I found this intangible hole in my heart from my father's absence, and it simply wouldn't go away.

As a young girl, I longed to find peace in my story but wasn't sure of where to find it in my heartache. I wanted to find peace in my pain, and that pain miraculously led me to find peace in Jesus.

I grew up in church learning about how God was my true Father on a rescue mission for my heart: His sacrifice on the cross, making a way for me to become His daughter and forgive all of the sin that had separated me from Him. I was delighted by this good news of the gospel: I had a perfect Heavenly Father who lavishly loved me to grant me the gift of an eternity with Him despite my rebellion and sin against Him. At the age of five, one summer evening, I knelt down with my mom beside my bed and asked Jesus to be my Savior and to receive the gift of my Father's love. That childlike prayer began a beautiful, redemptive adventure with my Father: a step-by-step journey of learning to trust Him to heal my heartbreak and fill the void of my father's absence. Over the years, I vividly witnessed God be faithful to His promise as Psalm 68:5 (NIV) declares, "A father to the fatherless...is God in His holy dwelling."

As a young girl, I loved talking to God all day about my joys and sorrows. I especially loved bedtime prayers as I knelt beside my bed with my mom. Most evenings, I fervently asked God to "give my mom a husband and a dad for me."

Year after year, I prayed. Year after year, I waited. Year after year, I kept asking God to do a miracle in changing my story. Yet He didn't change my story; I grew up without an earthly dad all those years.

As a young Christian woman, I still wrestled to find peace in my story of fatherlessness. I desperately tried to run away from facing the insecurity and hurt in my heart. I strove to be a high-achiever in every way: earning straight A's in classes and maintaining a "good-two-shoes" image as a peppy cheerleader in high school.

I was a good actress to myself and to others. I looked like a pretty and put-together Christian girl, but inwardly, my heart was shattered into pieces: insecure, fearful of rejection, and disillusioned with the twists and turns of my fatherless journey.

I began college and hit rock bottom emotionally and spiritually. I finally and fully faced the pain I had buried in my heart about an absent father. I grew weary of fearfully hiding from myself and God. The deep heartache of an absent father overwhelmed me. I found myself an utterly broken woman. I battled anxiety, shame, and an eating disorder. Amidst this brokenness, an undeniable blessing arose. The miraculous blessing was that I finally surrendered my whole heart and trusted God to be my Jehovah Rapha, "the God who heals."

In this sweet surrender, I poured out my entire heart to God through many tears, many prayers, many emotions, and many questions. And that made all the difference in my relationship with God in allowing Him to be the healer of my broken heart. I began fully trusting He would carry my storm-tossed heart through the waves of grief in my fatherless journey. This journey of trusting God led me down a path of healing from heartbreak: learning I could freely grieve with God and embrace His all-sufficient grace in my story.

In facing my deepest pain of father loss during college, I found a deeper peace in the refuge of God's steadfast presence as my faithful Father.

God's peace flooded my heart as I embraced His grace to face my heartbreak rather than run away from it. Inviting God into my grief became a sacred space of learning to trust in His goodness, celebrate His faithfulness, and accept His holy purposes for my suffering in the fatherless journey.

Over the course of several years in college, I dove deep into receiving God's fatherly love and His precious promises shared in the Bible. Countless prayers, innumerable tears, and many counseling sessions led me step- by-step in making peace with my pain: intimately knowing God as my true and trustworthy Father, who is always faithful to keep His promises and to give us His peace.

In college, I discovered one such promise described beautifully in Jeremiah 17:7-8 (NIV):

But blessed is the one who trusts in the LORD, whose confidence is in Him. They will be like a tree planted by the water that sends out its roots by the stream. It does not fear when heat comes; Its leaves are always green. It has no worries in a year of drought and never fails to bear fruit.

This scripture captivated my heart as I pondered the vivid picture it painted in my mind's eye: a fruitful tree flourishing amid drought, rooted in a nearby stream. And in that scripture, I saw my own journey with God through the "drought" of fatherlessness. Over the years, I had received the precious promise of His peace as my trust in the Lord deepened and was rooted in His promise to be a Father to my fatherless heart.

I remember sharing Jeremiah 17:7-8 as my "life verse" in an interview process to be a resident assistant in college. I was asked to describe my life experiences with God through a poster presentation, and this verse helped me do just that. I'll never forget drawing a brown tree trunk with its wispy roots extending into a blue stream and then sticking bright green, leaf-shaped sticky notes all along the branches. On each leaf, I wrote something about me: my favorite hobby, my life-shaping experiences, God's provisions in my life, and so on.

It was pure goodness for my heart to create this collage of God's grace: a tangible reminder of His faithfulness and His peace poured out through His undeniable presence in my life as my Heavenly Father.

As that young woman, I hadn't found peace in perfect circumstances. Rather, I received endless peace in embracing the unwavering presence of my perfect Father, who always keeps His promises. That timeless truth was true back then in college and still is now as I write these words as a middle-aged mother and wife. And this timeless truth remains for you and me in all seasons of our lives.

Our Father's steadfast presence truly promises that you and I can flourish in the peace of His sovereign, loving care amidst the adversity of battling father wounds in our hearts. We truly can find His peace in our pain through fully trusting God to be faithful to His promises.

The most undeniable expression of God's faithfulness to His promises lies in Jesus Christ, our victorious Savior, who forgives our sins and unconditionally loves us as children of God. 2 Corinthians 1:20 (NIV) shares, "For no matter how many promises God has made, they are 'Yes' in Christ." In light of what God has done for us in Jesus Christ, Hebrews 10:23 (NIV) challenges us to trust in God's faithfulness to keep all promises, as it says, "Let us hold unswervingly to the hope we profess, for he who promised is faithful."

What a comfort to know we can anchor our hearts in the unshakeable truth that God is faithful to His promises! He calls us to trust Him with our whole heart. We can strengthen our "trust muscles" by memorizing and meditating on His promises declared throughout the Bible. We truly become what we consistently behold. Thus, we must embrace God's truth to reign in our hearts to receive His peace, as Romans 8:6 (NIV) reminds, "...The mind governed by the Spirit is life and peace." Some ways I love to meditate on God's promises are playing worship music in the car, making Scripture the lock screen background on my phone, and displaying verses on my bathroom mirror. I simply want God's Word to be wherever I spend the most time, whether that be in the car or on my phone!

God's Word abounds with His promises to His people! I especially cherish the ones about the promise of peace for my heart that's been vulnerable to battles with anxiety and fear. I treasure the truth of Romans 5:1 (NIV) that declares, "Therefore, since we have been justified through faith, we have peace with God through our Lord Jesus Christ." This powerful promise reassures us that our faith in Jesus Christ grants us the precious gift of peace: a blessed serenity of your soul being rightly related to God and living joyously as His beloved daughter.

No longer an orphan, an unloved daughter, or an enemy of God. No, indeed! The grace of Jesus Christ pours out the endless gift of God's peace in our hearts as His daughters!

Therefore, we can continually receive our Father's peace by embracing it as a guaranteed gift to us as His daughters in our battles and trials in this life. God grants us a peace that overcomes amidst the suffering in our lives as Jesus promised in John 16:33 (NIV), "I have told you these things, so that in me you may have peace. In this world, you will have trouble. But take heart! I have overcome the world."

This overcoming peace from God is powerful and true, as I've witnessed it in my own journey of trusting God in a fatherless journey. God's peace has carried me and paved a path to being an overcomer in heartbreak!

I continue to learn that I can walk in God's peace through any painful or fearful circumstance. In those hard places, my temptation is to panic. But God's loving invitation is peace, as 1 Peter 5:7 (NIV) declares, "Cast all your anxiety on him because he cares for you."

Peace or panic. The choice is yours, and the choice is mine as to whether we will cling to fear or relinquish it, resting our hearts in God's continual care for us.

I admit that I still have my daily dose of battles with anxiety. The victory plan for this battle is declaring who God is to me in that battle zone of my anxious mind as I pray silently or out loud, "I cast my anxiety on You because You faithfully and perfectly care for me." Sometimes this prayer is quiet. Sometimes it's loud. Sometimes it's uttered slowly. Other times, it's whispered briefly while busily caring for my three boys.

God's peace floods my heart each and every time I pray and trust in His loving, sovereign care as my perfect Father.

As the prayers flow, so does God's peace fill my heart amidst whatever I'm facing in that moment.

God's peace is a guaranteed gift to us as our hearts are rooted deeply in trusting God to prove faithful in all circumstances. I love the way Philippians 4:7 (NIV) describes how God's peace protects our hearts when it promises, "And the peace of God, which transcends all understanding, will guard your hearts and minds in Christ Jesus." God's peace can be compared to a vigilant guard protecting the entry to a fortress. In the same way, His peace protects our hearts from being overcome by an attack of anxiety or fear.

Finally, we can walk in God's peace by accepting His eternal purpose for our sufferings as women with father wounds. I cherish this hope offered in 2 Corinthians 4:17 that reassures, "For our light and momentary troubles are achieving for us an eternal glory that outweighs them all." As such, we can rest our hearts in the promise that our suffering is not wasted in the loving hands of our faithful Father. He's using our journey with father wounds to deepen our faith in God's love and to prepare our hearts to spend an eternity with Him. And what reassurance that He pours out His peace in each step of faith in our journey homeward to heaven.

Rooted. That one word so perfectly describes where I want my heart to be, and where women like you and me can find lasting peace.

Rooted in trusting God: that's where you and I are promised to receive our Father's perfect peace. You and I may have found ourselves planted in a wasteland of heartbreak over father wounds. However, God meets us right there and promises to revive our hearts with His perpetual peace if we will trust Him to be faithful to His promises. Then our lives will be like a flourishing, fruitful tree rooted by a stream amidst a drought, as Jeremiah 17:7-8 (NIV) so vividly describes, "But blessed is the one who trusts in the Lord, whose confidence is in Him. They will be like a tree planted by the water that sends out its roots by the stream. It does not fear when heat comes; its leaves are always green. It has no worries in a year of drought and never fails to bear fruit."

Flourishing. Fruitful. Free of fear. That is our guaranteed destiny and journey in Jesus Christ as we root our hearts in the promises of our faithful Father.

Next Steps: Rooting Your Heart in Trusting God to Fulfill His Promises

1. Personalize the truth of Jeremiah 17:7-8. Create a picture of a tree with roots flowing into a nearby stream, labeled God's presence and promises. Write on the leaves of the tree specific ways God has been faithful to you, kept His promise, and has strengthened you to flourish amidst suffering in your life, particularly with father wounds.

2. Practice praying the promises of God. Whisper breath prayers based on these scriptures below. As you inhale, visualize yourself receiving God's peace as a protection over your heart and mind. As you exhale, visualize yourself releasing fear at God's throne of grace.

I cast all of my anxiety on You because You tenderly care for me as my good and faithful Father.

see 1 Peter 5:7

Father, I know Your name is a strong tower; I will run into it and always be safe.

see Proverbs 18:10

Father, You will keep my heart and mind in perfect peace as I trust in You.

see Isaiah 26:3

Father, I know I'll be blessed as I trust in Your unfailing love and unwavering faithfulness. I will not be overcome by fear. I will flourish in Your peace as I trust in You."

see Jeremiah 17:7-8

3. What truth about God as your Father will you embrace to receive His peace in your story of experiencing father wounds?

Chapter 4

Peace in the Middle of it All

By Dawn Fowler

When I think of peace, I think of serenity, calm, and stillness, like still waters with no movement. Peace can conjure different emotions, feelings, thoughts, and images. However, finding peace in the midst of chaos, confusion, and uncertainty is different. For many of us, finding peace amid chaos and uncertainty sometimes seems impossible, unreachable, and hard to attain. But if you have walked with God for any length of time, eventually you realize that peace comes from God. It comes from having a close, intimate, loving relationship with God, and that embodies the characteristics of our heavenly Father. Therefore, trying to find calm and stillness in any given moment can be difficult sometimes. In Matthew 19:26b (NIV) Jesus says, "With man this is impossible, but with God all things are possible."

When we take the time to reflect on scriptures like the one from Matthew, it reminds us of the importance of taking time in prayer, reading, or song to remember some of God's characteristics that bring about peace. God's unconditional love, Spirit, faithfulness, justice, patience, and other fruits of the Spirit gradually teach us how to be at peace in various situations and circumstances that can provoke fear, anger, confusion, or doubt. Anything in direct opposition to peace can make peace seem unattainable.

When I first started walking with God, I remember thinking, "Walking with God is too difficult." Specifically, I was faced with a handful of challenges that seemed insurmountable at the time. I was in college, working 20 to 30 hours a week, and had personal health issues, and relatives had health problems as well, and some of them died. It was a good time, but a time of great questioning of my faith and difficulty. I thought that I had done something wrong for all of this time to happen to me at the same time. Surprisingly, I had realized around this time that I was still grieving over the death of my father, who died when I was ten years old. Then, I thought about the following scripture, Philippians 4:7 (NKJV): "...And the peace of God, which surpasses all understanding, will guard your hearts and your minds in Christ Jesus." When I heard this scripture back in college, it brought comfort and a peace that words cannot explain. During that time, God helped me to understand the depth, width, and height of His unconditional love and peace. It brought about a sense of support, clarity, and direction.

There in that space in time that I found the power of God's love and unwavering peace. I am sure many of you can attest to the same thing. God's presence can be all-encompassing, and it shepherds you through challenging situations and circumstances. During this time, I learned to trust and believe in God's word. It did not come easily, but I gained a better understanding that His peace is not dependent on circumstances. Through every situation, God taught me to trust Him when I did not have everything I needed. Particularly, realizing that I did not have to have everything in order in my life to attain peace was liberating. This helped me let go of any preconceived notions I had about God and how He views all of us. Having the experience with God helped me understand that I did not need a designated space, place, or time to make time for God. Those times of prayer and worship with Him should help us throughout the day and throughout our lives. My purpose in sharing this with you is to encourage, build, and connect with others who have similar experiences. These experiences are meant to bring us closer to Christ and help us to have a clearer view of God in our lives. As time passes, our understanding deepens, and our relationship with God grows. Growth takes effect when you realize that peace and trust come from understanding who God is in your life and the circumstances you face.

The amazing thing about learning to find peace and trust beyond circumstances is that it helps us to surrender our weighted worries. Through many of life's twists and turns, learning to surrender everything to God can take time for some of us. It is when we learn to "let go and let God" that we learn the way of peace. There is something about learning to place everything on the altar without picking it up that changes our perspective on life and peace.

When you find peace and serenity in God, you gain a different perspective on life and your walk with God. Having peace does not mean you will always have ideal circumstances. This is what makes finding peace in God so miraculous: finding a level of peace and resolve that provides direction in many areas of our lives. Sometimes it is difficult to see this in our sometimes busy, chaotic world. For example, the issues I faced in college left me so fearful, doubtful, and confused that I almost dropped out.

But I was going to church with my mother, and at that time, that is where I found peace, love, and direction without judgment. Most importantly, having an amazing relationship with God helped me see this most clearly. Eventually, the fear, doubt, wrestling, and confusion dissipated, and God made everything clear enough for me to keep moving forward in my life. These are some of the reasons why finding peace is so crucial; it can help you to focus and function differently in your walk with God. Despite the challenges we encounter, you will gradually begin to realize that peace is not impossible or unreachable; it is attainable. Finding peace in God becomes everything: our foundation, our prayers, our vision, and our future. Rather than resorting to anything else, peace becomes your only option for a life filled with wholeness. It offers many of us the opportunity to gain a deeper understanding of God's unconditional love and peace in our lives. This allows you to help yourself and others as you continue to walk with God.

You will encounter challenges, but it will only push you closer to God and into complete surrender and wholeness with Him. It allows us to reconnect with God and to focus on what is most important. Once we understand the role that peace plays in our relationship with God, we can understand the gift of peace from Christ. John 14:27 (NIV) says, "Peace I leave with you; my peace I give you. Do not let your hearts be troubled and do not be afraid." Fortunately, God's unconditional love and compassion guide us through this process and help us to understand exactly what needs to be surrendered, resolved, and released. If there are things we are struggling with or grappling with, then we need to explore the reasons why. This is important because it can prevent many people from finding peace, and then it can become a hindrance. When you find peace and direction, God leads and guides you to where you need to be so He can bless you. The wonderful gift of peace brings clarity and a great sense of direction. Hopefully, if you have allowed God's gift of peace to unfold in your life, you will see it become your resting place. It will become a place for you to regroup and reflect as you move forward, and that is a gift. If you could see all of the fruits of the Spirit as gifts, it could enhance your overall view of your walk with God.

Peace, faith, and love help us to find a way during times of uncertainty and when we are feeling unsure about anything. Often, uncertainty and challenging times are the conditions that bring about a need for peace. You do not need peace if you have it, and you do not need happiness if you believe you have it. Basically, you begin to realize that the desire for peace stems from your need for it, and most of the transformation God brings about in your life comes from your need to change.

Personally, I had the experience of seeing my mother's health change dramatically before she made her transition.

This began in college until August 2022. After going through that experience for years, I learned the importance of peace amid juggling life obligations. While I was working and taking care of my children, I would help take care of her. It was hard at first, but God, family, and church taught me to see God's presence in my situation. We would sing songs together, pray, read the Bible with her, and spend quality time with her as a family. When we did those things as a family, it was such a huge blessing to all of us because it gave us a sense of strength, support, God's love, and compassion. We must remember that, in the midst of all the changes, God's loving presence and compassion are with us all. We are not exempt from negative feelings about our trials and tribulations. Fortunately, God understands that part of our walk with Him, and that is why we need to go to Him for everything.

Lastly, becoming peace carriers is a beautiful result of our peace walk with God. Once you understand the fruits of the spirit and the fruits being the light in the dark, everything becomes clearer. It states in John 1:7-9:

The same came for a witness, to bear witness of the Light, that all men through Him might believe. He was not that Light, but was sent to bear witness of that Light. That was the true Light, which lighteth every man that cometh into the world.

When I think of Jesus being the light in the darkness, it reminds me of Him walking on the water. The storms became calm because of Him. Therefore, my prayer for everyone reading this chapter is that you will find peace and God's unconditional love in His presence. We all face various situations, and some can be challenging, but I know that God will be with you through it all. Just hold on to His unchanging hand, and He will never let go of you. Knowing this should allow you to move through various situations with grace and peace, because many of them involve a level of complexity.

Chapter 5

Peace in the Chaos, in the Hurt, and in the Grief

By Karen Bedells

As we were leaving the cemetery after placing Christmas flowers on Daddy's grave, Mom started singing an old, familiar song from my childhood. The song was "Surely The Presence." I was only ten years old, but I vividly remember the times we sang that song in our small country Pentecostal church in Raymond, Mississippi. Our family, the Hills, started the church along with our pastor's family, the Nations. I remember truly feeling peace as we sang about the Lord's presence among us, the angel wings, and His glory shining on each face. As Momma's sweet, weakened voice sang, peace seemed to flow over us like still, quiet waters.

As odd as that all may sound, having peace in a cemetery, the peace that flowed out of her soul as she sang, made it immensely clear to me that when we have the peace of Jesus, it does not matter where we are or what circumstance we find ourselves in; we can remain at peace and feel His presence. "God's peace is perfect peace," momma said, "Quiet and restful". I am thankful to have come to know peace with Jesus as my personal savior.

Do you have His peace, perfect peace, quiet, and restful? Do you know Jesus as your Lord and Savior? The Bible tells us we can come to know Him by repenting of our sins and asking Him to be our Lord and Savior.

As His children, we can know that peace.

In reading a familiar scripture found in John 14:27-28, Jesus told us He would leave *His* peace for us! That scripture specifically says it is *His* peace that *He* gives us, not peace that the world would be able to provide, but peace that only *He* can give. In plain English with a Southern girl's twist, not as the world gives, y'all, He gives something different! What my Savior and friend Jesus says is plain and simple. He is the one who gives us peace. *He* is the one who gives us peace! In the South, we draw things out.... We speak a little slower, and we may repeat ourselves a bit. We may just sit right down by the fire, inside or outside, close our eyes, and embrace the moments. So, bear with me as we just sit for a minute.

Close your eyes for a minute and imagine sitting in front of a slow-burning fire in an old homeplace, quiet and serene with only the crackling of the fire breaking the silence. Sit quietly on the floor in front of the fire as if to prop up against grandmother's old, worn rocking chair, where she sat to read The Word to her grandchildren so many times. The fire is warm on your toes. Her words warm in your heart. The firewood that came fresh out of the woodshed (dried out, of course, because that's how our parents and grandparents taught us) is popping as the fire catches on to each carefully split piece of wood.

This reminds me of a peace I felt as a young girl growing up on the homestead. I loved being outside. I loved going to ride the fence line with daddy or squirrel hunting. When we would prepare for winter, we cut firewood right off of those very fence lines. When I was with my daddy chopping the firewood, I had comfort, a peace, or so I thought. That peace only lasted while we chopped wood. It was only in the moment. A comfort in the moment. But oh, the peace that our heavenly Father gives is not just in the moment; it is a lasting peace. He gives us peace in the chaos, in the hurt, and in the grief. So, from this Southern girl's heart, just in case you need to hear it again, close your eyes again and recite those words until your heart hears it, "Peace I leave with you, my peace I give unto you: not as the world giveth, give I unto you. Let not your heart be troubled, neither let it be afraid" (John 14:27-28).

Do you seek this peace? Do you know Jesus? To have peace, that only *He* gives, we must be His. John 16:33 (NKJV) speaks this so clearly, "These things I have spoken to you, that in Me you may have peace. In the world you will have tribulation; but be of good cheer; I have overcome the world." In this tribulation (in chaos, in hurt, and in grief), this verse is so comforting, helping us know we have the peace of Jesus. The journey to true peace begins with knowing Jesus Christ as your Savior. After becoming *His,* then we can seek the peace that is ours *in* Him. Being in Him means we are united with Him. In Him (forgiven, renewed, set apart), we are a new creature, forgiven of our sins when we repent and ask Jesus to be Lord and Savior of our lives. We receive the Holy Spirit, who is our comforter and gives us strength to live as Christians and followers of Jesus as He has called us to live. Being in Christ is a continually growing relationship in which we increase in our faith and deepen our walk with Him and *in Him.* Are you living in Him? My friend, this is where we have that peace, *in Him. Oh, the peace we have in Him in our chaos, in our hurt, and in our grief.*

A few years ago, I did a Bible study on Psalms 23 by Jennifer Rothschild, *Psalms 23 The Shepherd Within Me*, which I would highly recommend. Who would have thought you could do an entire six-week Bible study on Psalms 23! Oh, one seeking Him, that is just how important that chapter is and contains such goodness to bless us in our daily walk. As I read through my notes written on each page, having my thoughts focused on peace and all that it means to have peace, or even to understand what peace is or where it even comes from, I started reading Psalms 23:1: "The Lord is my shepherd; I shall not want." If I am living *in Him,* He *IS MY* shepherd. **When we are complete in *Him,* we want nothing, "Because we have all we need in our Shepherd"** (Rothschild). We have peace in our Shepherd. Psalms 23:2 goes on to say, "He maketh me to lie down in green pastures: He leadeth me beside the still waters". Our Shepherd leads us to rest and experience the peace we have *in Him;* He gives us provision in the peace we have *in*

Him. He restoreth my soul. Yes! We are restored with the peace we have *in Him.* This whole chapter speaks peace to my heart, and I pray you will never read it the same again. Grasp the peace that He provides for us, His children, in the chaos, in the hurt, and in the grief.

The Bible tells us we will have troubles, chaos, hurt, and grief. He will be with us when we are His, and we will have His peace in those troubling times. I have come to know this peace personally. I have experienced grief throughout my life in the death of loved ones so close to my heart. At the age of thirteen, I lost my oldest sister. She was sixteen years old. This was devastating to our family. Although I had been taught faith my whole life, I had become a Christian about four months before that sad, Thanksgiving Day car wreck that took my sister's life. Only the peace of Jesus saw us through that time and in the years to come. So many times since then, with the death of family and friends, I have clung to so many scriptures that assure us of the peace we have in Jesus. I found peace in the hurt.

Now, walking through grief with my precious nephew and his family, after being a Christian for forty-five years, I am still experiencing the peace of Jesus, although days are hard and we don't understand. And I have to admit, we question God with why. To describe the chaos, the hurt, and the grief, I share my personal walk with the cancer diagnosis of my nephew. After being married for 19 years to the love of her life, best friend, goofy "traffic guy at church," my nephew's wife, a young mother and wife, found herself looking at the MRI scan glowing with a bright light. A hot spot: something that should not be there! As her face, heart, and body literally shook, she crumbled into that strong embrace from the man she adored and cherished. She heard the devastating news. It was deafening. Glioblastoma is a death sentence, especially as she knew it with the death of her father-in-law just a decade ago.

Eight months later, my precious niece, Kemily, and nephew, Reed, whose walk with the Lord I admire greatly, had walked through many battles: the diagnosis, the brain biopsy, the harsh radiation, the repeated chemo, missing out on summer fun with the twins, the seizures, and even more. In the grief, her face lit up when we talked about peace! Her tired face shone with a glow, her eyes sparkled, and with her lips forming a discreet smile, she formed the word peace. "Peace", she said, "It's just trusting and abiding (in Him)! You're helpless, and you're ok with it!" In the words of my 41-year-old nephew, Reed, "We are dealing hope to others, just one beggar telling another beggar where to find bread." Truly a picture of the "Peace of God which passeth all understanding," we cling to in difficult times, which goes on to say, "shall keep your hearts and minds through Christ Jesus" (Philippians 4:7). Sitting by my nephew's bed in hospice, the peace of Jesus was present. In Jesus, I found peace in the grief.

Grasping all that Jesus left us in His word to lead us and guide us through such difficulties in life, as he told us we would, is a daily walk and practice to build our faith and enjoy the peace we have in Him.

Peace is one of the fruits of the Spirit. When we have that spirit dwelling in us as we live in Him, we have that fruit, and we begin to bear that fruit to share with others.

When I started graduate school for my master's degree in nursing in August 2013, after graduating from nursing school 26 years prior, I knelt by the bed and prayed for the Lord to give me a scripture to hang on to for strength for the next two years! Sitting in my hotel room in Natchez, Mississippi, overlooking the vast Mississippi River, having my quiet time with the Lord that morning before classes started, He gave me this scripture! Psalm 29:11, "The Lord will give strength unto his people, the Lord will bless his people with peace."

We must *be His* to glean from His promises; as *His children, we* are blessed with His peace. This scripture proved to be just what I needed! In times of stress, worry, and fret, I had His promise of peace and strength! I found peace in the chaos. We must *be His* to glean from His promises. Many times, I have been reminded of this scripture and His faithfulness. Even now, as I read this scripture, having just finished my morning cup of coffee, it is as if I am having coffee with an old friend, with this scripture warming my heart. With the peace He promised He would give to *His* people, oh, the peace my precious Lord has given me then and so many times since through His word, through prayer, through others speaking into my life, and even through the difficult times, God has allowed me to be filled with His peace, because I am His.

Talking with my close friends, who I am so blessed to call sisters in the Lord, we were sharing about peace. The wisdom they shared in their thoughts resonated with my heart and reflected the word of the Lord. (Surround yourself with a community of dear friends who speak Jesus into your life; friends who hold you up when you are weak, or who will lower you through the roof to get you to Jesus). One precious friend shared her thoughts on peace with me. Peace is something we have inside of us, which keeps us calm in the storms around us.

Although we may lose the stillness and quietness we crave, the peace never leaves us when we are His children, when we complete ourselves in Him.

We may feel that peace has left us in moments of chaos, hurt, and grief, but clinging to the scriptures tells us that His peace transcends all understanding. In fact, the Bible mentions peace over 400 times, emphasizing the importance of embracing the peace we have *in Him*. In Hebrew, the word for peace is "Shalom."

Shalom refers to the wholeness and completeness we have in a flourishing relationship with God; peace equals wholeness and completeness. Read that again! When I asked my darling youngest daughter, Bari Katilyn, what peace meant to her, she shared Philippians 4:6-7 with me as her go-to scripture for peace. "Be careful for nothing; but in every thing by prayer and supplication with thanksgiving let your requests be made known unto God." We talked for a minute and agreed that when we are complete in Him, we can bring our requests and thanksgiving before Him. We can have calm instead of chaos, healing instead of hurting, and comfort instead of grief. We can have peace. She shared with me, " The Lord provides peace when the world around us is full of anger, anxiety, worry, and fear. He is our Shalom." I agree, baby girl! I agree! And y'all, Isaiah 9:6 tells us He is the "Prince of Peace!" He is our savior, He is our Lord, He is our Shalom, He is our Prince of Peace.

In the chaos, in the hurt, and in the grief, He is our Prince of Peace. As I shared immense grief with my sister-in-love, my mother's heart hurt for her. Caring for her oldest son, plagued with an aggressive cancer, losing her husband to the same cancer ten years before, my sister-in-love, Tori, shares, "Peace is a feeling I get that is calm, trusting, and palpable to me. The peace I have cannot be explained. All I know is when I choose to give thanks to God for His faithfulness and mercy, and when I think about the goodness He has brought to my life, I don't have much time for worry. Some of my favorite life verses are found in Philippians 4:6-8. In my walk with Jesus, I have found that if I act on those verses, I experience true peace." My precious next-to-youngest daughter, Natalie, shared with me as we were discussing peace, "Peace means rest for my soul, with all of the stress and worry, my soul still gets to rest *in Him* because only God can give us that peace". Amen, sweet girl! I need that rest in His peace. In life and in death, in chaos and in hurt and in grief, only God can give us that peace when we are His, when we are completely His.

One of my favorite scriptures is Psalms 37:4, "Delight thyself also in the LORD, and he shall give thee the desires of thine heart." Delight yourself in Him, complete yourself in Him, fulfill yourself in Him. Not in the things the world offers: success, climbing the ladder, fame, fortune, but fulfill yourself in Him. Allow him to complete you! Align yourself with His divine will. Friend, as you surrender to Him, He can begin to fill those areas of your life that you have filled with everything but Him. He will order your steps and direct your paths through the peace He provides for you. One of my favorite scriptures and my next-to-oldest, dear daughter Maegan's, favorite is Proverbs 3:5-6, "Trust in the LORD with all thine heart; and lean not unto thine own understanding. In all thy ways acknowledge Him, and He shall direct thy paths." Yes Mae! If we can acknowledge Him in all things, we can walk the path He sets before us to complete ourselves in Him.

As we pray for Him to direct our paths, surrendering all to Him, becoming His children, completing ourselves in Him, we begin to relinquish the chaos, the hurt, the grief. We exchange that for the peace we have in Him. Sydney, my sweet, oldest daughter, had such a beautiful hymn played at her wedding: "Be Thou My Vision." This beautiful song repeatedly proclaims the message that only in You Lord, do I need dwelling in me. I need you first, Lord, and no matter what comes my way, Lord, keep my vision on you. Wow Syd! What a proclamation to make. Be my vision, Lord, first and foremost. Again, we repeat ourselves a little bit in the South, so I will take advantage of that heritage to say again, when we are in Him, *when we are in Him*, when He is first in our lives, when He only is our vision, when we complete ourselves in Him, when we find that true rest in Him, we find His peace that we have in Him. I have found this to be true so many times in life through the chaos, in the hurt, and in the grief.

As I watched my elderly momma, who committed years to the care of my daddy, their congregation, and family, walking in the Proverbs 31 way, I saw a peace that she had in her heart. When we talked about that peace, she spoke words so soothing to my soul. Her very soft, now weakened voice from strokes and dementia, still speaks so loudly, sharing God's peace in her life, "God's peace is perfect peace! Quiet and restful!" When Daddy died, we grieved. We were so sad. But that unwavering peace sustained us and still does today. I see that same peace in a retired minister, my pastor growing up, whose health has been failing, but continues to care for his elderly wife. He explained peace so simply yet so powerfully, "Peace: absence of all worries." I closed my eyes after hearing those words; it was involuntary, as if the Holy Spirit allowed that quiet, restful peace to wash over me and resonate with my spirit. Oh, how soothing it was to bask in His peace, in the presence of Jesus. Even now, having lived through chaos, hurt, and grief myself, I close my eyes and share this with you. Whatever is troubling your spirit, your soul, your mind, your body, allow Him to fill you with that "peace that passes all understanding". Allow the rest you find in His peace to heal your tired and weakened soul. Embrace the Holy Spirit and allow yourself to be consumed in Him. Surrender all. Receive Him. Receive His peace.

Daniel was grounded in that peace in the lion's den. He had surrendered all to his God. He was His Lord's and His Lord was His. He had received that peace in his God. He did not fear what was around him. He knew that perfect peace. He knew his God was in control. Recently, on a plane ride to Charlotte, North Carolina, the winds blew, and the plane became turbulent. The pilot came over the intercom and announced that the attendants would take their seats for now. He spoke calmly and without concern. He knew he was in control of the plane and had no fear. I truly did not even think about the turbulence. The captain, the pilot, was in control of the plane. I was not fearful. But more so than that, *I knew* who was *really* in charge of the winds. I had no fear. Unlike the young man sitting next to me, who became quite worried. Peace is like riding on that airplane with turbulence along the way and not worrying, reading your book, enjoying the clouds or sunshine looking out of the window, trusting the captain who is in control of the plane, just as we should sit back and relax when turbulence hits us in life.

Our Lord is in control of the chaos, in the hurt, and in the grief. We can rest and sleep in the turbulence. Jesus slept during the storm with his disciples, fretting and becoming so fearful. The chaotic winds hit their boat on their journey on the sea, and the disciples panicked. But Jesus was asleep. Mark 4: 36-41 recounts this story. In Mark 4:39-41, we read how Jesus calmed the "And he arose, and rebuked the wind, and said unto the sea, Peace, be still. And the wind ceased, and there was a great calm. And he said unto them, why are ye so fearful? How is it that ye have no faith?" With the peace of Jesus, we can relax in the chaos and have no fear. We can proclaim His words, "Peace be still."

My friends, this peace we speak of is an important part of our faith journey. It's truly a "peace that passes all understanding." Philippians 4:7, "And the *peace of God* which passeth all understanding, shall keep your hearts and minds through Christ Jesus"(emphasis added). Peace is not something we have to fight to maintain due to the stressors and struggles of this world (I must admit I originally wrote 'peace is something we must fight to maintain,' but no, we don't have to fight to keep that peace). When we are His, we have that peace, and as His children, nothing can steal that. We have it!! *In Him* we have that peace even in chaos, even in hurt, and even in grief. Peace is a gift to us when we are His. We live in a world that constantly challenges us with fear, bitterness, and worry, stemming from the evil in our imperfect world. But we can hold onto the perfect peace which comes from our God, our Savior, Christ Jesus. By keeping our minds "stayed" on him, we win the battle in our mind, in spiritual warfare, and in all areas of our lives, even our physical well-being. However, when we allow our minds, hearts, and souls to be filled with other things and do not have that daily walk with the Lord, our peace becomes distant, as does our relationship with the Lord. We must live our lives in Him. We must bear the fruits of the spirit. A tree is known by the fruits it bears.

This scripture in Philippians clearly tells us that the peace of God keeps our hearts and minds through Christ! He guards our hearts and minds. Wow, how powerful peace is! We must take time to be still, take time to trust, and take time to remember his faithfulness through each valley and storm to grasp how strong our peace is in times of distress. "Thou wilt keep him in perfect peace, whose mind *is stayed on thee:* because he trusteth in thee" (Isaiah 26:3). Keep your mind stayed on Him even in times of distractions in the chaos, in the hurt, and in the grief. My husband of thirty-six years, Barry, has a favorite verse in Isaiah 40:31 which tells us, "But They that wait upon the Lord (we are still before Him, we are yearning for His presence, His will, His plan- we are simply waiting, and by doing so) shall renew their strength; they show mount up with wings as Eagles; they shall run (be made strong), and not be weary (have rest); and they shall walk, and not faint (we will preserve through the storms)" (my notes added). In Him we are renewed, refreshed, strengthened, and blessed with peace. In Him.

In Numbers chapter 6, we see the Lord speaking to Moses to charge the children of Israel to be separated from the world and completely committed to the Lord, to be *in Him.* Numbers 6:2 says, "Speak unto the children of Israel, and say unto them, when either man or woman shall separate themselves to vow a vow of a Nazarite, to separate themselves unto the Lord." This story goes on to describe in great detail the charge that is placed on them to commit themselves to the Lord, completely. That came with a cleansing of the heart, the soul, and the mind. And oh, the beauty in verse 26, where we see the blessing due them when following after the Lord! We again see where we are blessed with peace when we commit ourselves to the Lord and honor Him with our lives, being separated from the worldly things that try to entice us and fill our hearts and minds. "The Lord lift up His countenance on thee and bless thee with peace". Just as we have seen in scriptures, when we come to know Him as Savior and Lord, when we complete ourselves *in Him*, when we hide His words in our hearts, we truly have the blessing of peace. The blessing of peace that Mom and I shared in the cemetery that day.

"Peace Garden" was the sign I saw as we came down the poorly paved, bumpy road through the mountainous cemetery in Hot Springs, Arkansas. I missed that sign driving into the cemetery. It was not a coincidence that I missed it, but rather our Heavenly Father was waiting to speak to me, having my heart prepared to receive what He would say to me. My focus as I was driving into the cemetery was task-oriented, mission-focused, getting those flowers placed perfectly in the crooked vase on daddy's grave marker. Distracted, I was focused on my itinerary and missed the peace along the way. It was dreadfully cold that day, and I knew Mom would need to sit in the car as I gathered the fading Thanksgiving flowers and maybe place them on a grave without flowers. My sisters, Kim and Charlie, and I share flowers to bless others, whose family may not get to visit their loved one's grave.

As we left Daddy's grave, feeling as if we had visited him, Mom and I prayed as we always do. Then she began to sing that oh so familiar song about the presence of the Lord. A spirit of worship filled the car. Our hearts came before the Lord in worship, not realizing we were preparing our hearts to receive His word, the very word I had been praying about, peace! As I sang with momma, the Holy Spirit, our comforter from Jesus, filled our hearts with praise. The Bible tells us in Psalms 22:3, "But thou art holy, O thou that inhabitest the praises of Israel." In plain English, He inhabits the praise of His people. We praised, and He was surely with us. John 14:27 then tells us Jesus gives us that peace, not peace that the world gives, but His peace. He was with us that day in the cemetery and gave us His peace. My heart being prepared to receive that peace, offering Him praise and worship, and putting my plan aside, allowed me to hear His Word and know truly that *in Him*, we have peace. I smiled, knowing Jesus had just walked with us in the cemetery.

An Invitation:

Do you find yourself seeking peace? Do you feel empty? Have you truly just surrendered your all to Him, to be complete in Him? If not, to know Jesus and know His peace, repent of your sins, ask Jesus to be Lord of your life, and trust him as your Savior. This is the first step in having this peace in Jesus and living in life as an overcomer through Jesus. Publicly professing that faith in Baptism shares our faith that we are His and He is ours. Just place your hands out, palm up, to receive from him the peace in the chaos, in the hurt, and in the grief. Just physically lay all of your burdens at His feet and fill yourself with the peace we have *in Him.* Rest in His presence. John 16:33 affirms that our peace is in Jesus, "These things I have spoken unto you, that in me ye might have peace. In the world ye shall have tribulation: but be of good cheer; I have overcome the world." He has overcome the chaos. He has overcome the hurt. He has overcome the grief. Walking daily in His Word and spending time in prayer, our faith is built through that personal relationship with Jesus. He becomes our Shepherd, and in growing that relationship with Jesus, we lean in and complete ourselves in Him. May He walk with you, too, my friends, may you come to know Him and know His peace that we can have when we are His. May His "Grace and peace be multiplied unto you through the knowledge of God and Jesus our Lord" (2 Peter 1:2).

Chapter 6

Moving from Anxiety to Peace: Jesus' Invitation to a New Way of Being

By Julie Baldwin

THEREFORE, DO NOT BE ANXIOUS, SAYING, 'WHAT SHALL WE EAT?' OR 'WHAT SHALL WE DRINK?' OR 'WHAT SHALL WE WEAR?' FOR THE GENTILES SEEK AFTER ALL THESE THINGS, AND YOUR HEAVENLY FATHER KNOWS THAT YOU NEED THEM ALL.
MATTHEW 6:31-32, ESV

Flashes of light filled the night sky, lighting up my room. Thunder rolled, and rain began to patter on the corrugated roof of my family home. My eyes popped open. I lay there listening intently. Was it coming towards us? Was the rain getting heavier? I didn't move, but all my senses were alert. I could hear the wind howling through the trees outside my window, and then the rain started getting heavier, bashing against the roof. It didn't stop, but I prayed that it would. It kept pounding. My stomach clenched tight; all my muscles were taut, my heart beat faster, and the fear rose inside me. "God, please make it stop!" I would pray over and over.

Finally, I couldn't stand it anymore. I ran into my parents' room, woke them, and warned them of the impending doom. If it rained too much too quickly, the stormwater drain couldn't cope, and we'd get a flash flood through the back of our house. I hated it when that happened. They got up, lifted the washing machine onto bricks to protect it, and quickly picked things up off the floor before the water came. I sat frozen with fear. Then, the water rushed forcefully through the back of our house, rising a step, then another. Just when I thought it would reach me, it began to recede.

After the water had receded, my mum would take me back to bed and console me, but the pattern was there. As I grew older, anxiety and fear seemed to follow me and would overtake me, affecting me mentally, emotionally, and physically. I always felt somewhat ashamed and embarrassed by my feelings, as if they were something I needed to hide.

Most people experience fear or anxiety in their lives and sometimes it can feel overwhelming. Have you ever felt anxious or filled with worry over something that may or may not happen?

You might find yourself anxious over making the right decision for your future career, which job you should take - is this the path I should take, or this one? Perhaps you might feel anxious over relationships in your life- maybe it's the next family gathering, especially if there are tensions in your relationships. You might feel anxious about getting up in front of others and presenting a talk. Or you might feel anxious over your finances- do I have enough to pay my bills?

There are so many things about our lives and our world that can make us feel anxious and lead us to fear and worry.

Yet Jesus says that if we are following Him and His Kingdom way, then there is no need to be anxious, there is no need to worry. Imagine it- no need to worry! This seems astounding to me and, in fact, it seems unachievable but in the gospel of Matthew Jesus invites us into a way of life that is not fixed on the troubles of the here and now but one that is postured towards a kingdom perspective where there is no need to be anxious, especially about the basic things of life- what we eat & drink, and what we wear.

Jesus offers us, especially those of us who are prone to worry, anxiety, and fear, some invitations to help us to move out of anxiety and towards peace and actually become people of peace in the world around us. Let's take a look at what He invites us to do.

Invitation 1: Remind yourself that God is your provider

Look at the birds of the air: they neither sow nor reap nor gather into barns, and yet your heavenly Father feeds them. Are you not of more value than they? And which of you by being anxious can add a single hour to his span of life?

Matthew 6:26-27, ESV

In these verses, Jesus tells us that what we look at determines what our inner life is like. When you feel anxious, where are you looking? Usually it is inwardly. We embody anxiety. I feel it in my gut, my knees shake, my hands are sweaty, and my heart rate rises. What is it like for you? We can so easily become stuck within ourselves, but Jesus says, instead of looking inward, change the direction of your gaze! He says to look outward, and He uses birds to help us to do that.

I love watching birds. I have a family of wrens that visit my garden every morning and bring me joy. When I first moved into a new estate nine years ago, most of the trees had been cleared. The only bird that was around was the Willy Wagtail. Though they are little, they are tough little birds. But over time, as the trees have grown and people have planted gardens, a variety of birds have appeared.

As I have watched them, I have noticed some things about birds. Firstly, I notice that each one knows where to go to find food. God has somehow planted within them the understanding of how to find the food they need as they travel among the plants that are in flower at different times. And the other thing I notice is that there is abundance in God's garden in every season for them all to be satisfied. Different trees flower at different times to provide food for birds year-round.

Jesus is saying to learn from them! Birds are not anxious about their next meal; they are not trying to control it, and they don't store food away so that they will be sure they have some for tomorrow. No, each day they go out expecting to find food, and each day God provides it for them.

Jesus reminds us that we, too, are creatures; we are not the Creator, we are not God, though we often try to be God and find ourselves trying to control our lives and the situations we find ourselves in. But we are not God, only He is in charge:

He is sovereign. That means that He has supreme power and authority over all creation, including us.

God is not only sovereign but also compassionate. He made us and knows what we need, and He makes it available to us in every season of our lives. In the Old Testament (Genesis 22:14), Abraham named Him "Jehovah Jireh," which means "my provider." As we look at the birds, we can see the provision of a loving Creator, our provider. This is who He is to the birds and to us.

So here's a question for us to sit with and ponder:

Do I trust that God is in control and that He will provide for me?

Or do I feel that I have to make it happen for myself, that somehow, I am better at being God than He is. I'm not saying that we don't have our part to play; of course, we do. Even the birds have to fly to where the food is. It doesn't just come to them, but each of those birds expects that what they need is there for them- that's the difference. And this is to be the posture of a person following the way of the King, one who lives with the expectation that God is compassionate toward us and will provide for us.

Invitation 2: Understand how valuable you are to God

The second invitation that Jesus wants us to use focuses on who we are to Him. He says to us, "Are you not of more value than they?" Matthew 6:26b, ESV

Jesus reminds us that we are valuable to God, even more valuable than the birds whom He amply provides for. You are valuable to God! That is the truth about who you are. I wonder if that is actually what you believe about yourself? It is so easy for us to notice all the things about us that make us unworthy of God's love and attention, but God says that you are of infinite worth to Him.

As we look at the birds, we are reminded of who God is: He is our loving provider, but we are also reminded of who we are: we are valuable to Him. If He looks after birds, He will look after us.

To reinforce this truth, Jesus then turns to the wildflowers out in the field.

I love going outside and looking at my garden, seeing which plants are in flower, pulling some weeds, and watering the plants. My garden is full of color because I love flowers, and I love the joy that my garden brings me. It is one of my spiritual practices to be in my garden because it is there, amongst God's creation, that I feel a connection with God, I slow down, I get lost in the beauty around me, and I spend time in God's presence. It is a great way to lower the feeling of stress or anxiety. And it is flowers that Jesus brings into our view to notice something deeper about who He is and who we are.

> And why are you anxious about clothing? Consider the lilies of the field, how they grow: they neither toil nor spin, yet I tell you, even Solomon in all his glory was not arrayed like one of these. But if God so clothes the grass of the field, which today is alive and tomorrow is thrown into the oven, will he not much more clothe you, O you of little faith?
>
> Matthew 6:28-30, ESV

Jesus asks us to consider the lilies of the field, and he points us to Solomon, who was one of the richest Kings in Israel's history. With great wealth, Solomon could dress himself in the finest of clothes. And Jesus compares him in all his rich adornment to the simple wildflowers out in the field: flowers that are here today and gone tomorrow.

A bunch of flowers can remind someone that you love them, they can fill a room with color and perfume, and they can bring joy and delight. But... a bowl of them won't satisfy our hunger, and we can't use them for fuel. In fact, the only purpose they have is to look good for a little while. Flowers don't last; in a week, they are ready to be thrown in the bin.

Yet God created each flower with such intricacy, each uniquely different, and Jesus is telling us that if God spends so much time creating and designing flowers that don't last long and that have little purpose, how much more will He care for you. **You are worth so much more than flowers.**

So, here's another question for you to sit with and ponder:

Do I believe that I am valuable to God?

I mean, really believe. Or do I believe that maybe God just has to love me because that's who He is, that He just has to put up with me? Or do I really believe in the depths of my being that I am valuable to Him? Because that is the truth. My worth to Him is immeasurable. Being valued is a core need we all have- we want to know that we are important to someone, but we often look for our value from those around us. But Jesus reminds us that we are valuable to God, and that He is the source and supplier who fills the need we have.

Believing this truth is where we find our security and confidence when we are tempted to worry or become anxious. Building on this foundation, Jesus then issues a deeper challenge for us that hits right at our hearts.

Invitation 3: Seek first His Kingdom

I don't know about you, but sometimes we can doubt His care for us, and we can turn to worry instead of God. God says to us, "O you of little faith" (Matthew 6:30b, ESV). This is not just a pithy phrase or a pointed rebuke; Jesus is going to the heart of the issue. Because at the heart of worry and anxiety is distrust of God's provision for you and distrust of your worth to God. It is a faith issue, and He calls it out and summons us to action. He calls us to live out what we know to be true, trusting God to do what He says He will do and living a life that shows that.

As I've grown to know Him more over the years, I have come to know a God who is kind and compassionate. So when those times come where the anxiety rises in me, I pause, take some deep breaths, and remind myself of who He is- a loving, compassionate God, and then I remind myself of who I am in Him - valuable! As I spend some time focusing on this, the anxiety settles within me, and my soul can rest in Him.

We can have confidence in Him because we know He loves us, we are valuable to Him, and He is capable of knowing and providing what we need. So, He says, **'Trust me. I've got it.'** Live a life that shows you know this to be true.

Jesus reminds us again in Matthew 6:32-32, ESV:

Therefore, do not be anxious, saying, 'What shall we eat?' or 'What shall we drink?' or 'What shall we wear?' For the Gentiles seek after all these things, and your heavenly Father knows that you need them all.

He is saying that there are two ways of being: the Gentile's way, that is, those who live anxious lives because they only trust in themselves, and the way of the King, where we actively live in the truth that the King is good and He will provide and care for us, and we can trust Him because we are valuable to Him.

How do we do that? Jesus invites us to seek Him first.

But seek first the kingdom of God and his righteousness, and all these things will be added to you. "Therefore, do not be anxious about tomorrow, for tomorrow will be anxious for itself. Sufficient for the day is its own trouble.

Matthew 6:33-34 ESV

A person who seeks God's kingdom first is someone who has his or her priorities in order; they direct their focus away from themselves and onto Jesus. They are not going to be focused on the worries of this life, but instead they will focus on God's Kingdom and trust that He will provide all that they need in this life. To seek the kingdom means that you will desire things the way God wants, rather than what you want.

Think about what it would look like for you to do this in every area of your life. Instead of worrying, what does it look like to seek him first in your relationships, your marriage, your kids, your family, your friendships (especially the ones that are challenging)? For me, it's committing them to Him, knowing that they are more valuable to Him than to me, as much as I might love them, and that helps me to trust God in the ways that He will work in their lives to draw them to Himself.

A Person of Peace

Paul also reminds us in Philippians 4:6-7 (ESV) to not be anxious.

> Do not be anxious about anything, but in everything by prayer and supplication with thanksgiving let your requests be made known to God. And the peace of God, which surpasses all understanding, will guard your hearts and your minds in Christ Jesus."

This is what we are all after, aren't we? Peace! Peace in our homes, peace in our workplaces, peace in our church, peace in all our relationships. And for those who choose to follow Jesus, who call on His name, who seek first His kingdom, they have access to peace. And not just a surface peace but a deep, lasting peace, peace that doesn't make sense to those who live in our anxious, driven world. Peace that protects us and guards our hearts and our minds in Christ Jesus.

When we seek Him first, we can live as a person of peace, a non-anxious presence in the world, who can stay calm in the storm of anxiety around us. They are a person who does not become anxious when things don't go to plan. They don't absorb other people's anxiety either. They remain non-anxious despite the circumstances.

Do you know people like this?

Imagine a world where more of Jesus' followers were marked by inner peace and brought a non-anxious presence into the anxious world around them. These people would live distinctly different from the culture around them, where the common state of being is anxious. What a different world it would be.

These people have such a strong faith in God and trust in Him that they embody peace in all areas of their lives. They are the person of peace at a contentious family gathering. They are a person of peace in a harried school pickup zone. They are a person of peace in a workplace filled with conflict. They are a person of peace at the local kids' soccer game or the slow-moving grocery line. This type of presence in our world is noticed, and it tells people whether a life following Jesus is worth pursuing.

Jesus, of course, is the ultimate non-anxious presence. In the Gospels, we read how he faced chaotic situations and encountered difficult people without letting anything control his feelings. He did not get anxious when others did, and he did not absorb other people's anxiety.

We read of an incident that reveals this in Matthew 8:23-27 (ESV):

And when he got into the boat, his disciples followed him. And behold, there arose a great storm on the sea, so that the boat was being swamped by the waves; but he was asleep. And they went and woke him, saying, "Save us, Lord; we are perishing." And he said to them, "Why are you afraid, O you of little faith?" Then he rose and rebuked the winds and the sea, and there was a great calm. And the men marveled, saying, "What sort of man is this, that even winds and sea obey him?

So how do we become a non-anxious presence like Jesus was in the world we live in now, in the family we are part of, in the place where we work, in the neighbourhood we live in, or in our church?

Jesus tells us that the answer lies in seeking Him first, allowing His rule and reign over our lives. It's fixing our gaze on Him every day and actively choosing to trust Him because He is our compassionate provider, and we are valuable to Him. As we pursue a life with Him in charge, we can enjoy His non-anxious presence in our lives, and we can, in turn, become a non-anxious presence in the lives of others.

I no longer feel anxious when storm clouds appear; instead, they remind me of God's power to provide for us during life's storms.

I also love that Jesus directs our gaze to the simplest and most common things, like birds or flowers. No matter where you live in the world, you can look up and find a bird in the sky and find flowers even growing out of the cleft of a rock or in a desert. The next time you see one, let it be an invitation to know that God is your provider and He will provide what you need, and to understand how valuable you are to God. Let it remind you that He is God, and He is in control, and His invitation to you is to seek Him first.

As you release the anxiety and welcome His peace, you get to take that peace everywhere you go into a world that desperately needs it

Your challenge for this week:

Take some time outside in God's creation and look up at any birds you see. Pause for a moment and remind yourself that God is present with you and He will provide what you need in whatever situation you are worrying about. Then look at the flowers (even if it's just a pot plant). Remind yourself that just as flowers are beautiful and God made them, He sees you as <u>much more</u> valuable than they are! Remind yourself that you are valuable to Him by saying it out loud - "I am valuable to God!" (Repeat it until it starts to take hold in your heart)

Then take three deep breaths: as you breathe out, breathe out your worry and anxiety, and as you breathe in, breathe in His love for you. You can trust Him with your life because He knows what you need.

As you turn your gaze to Jesus and put Him first ahead of all your worries, welcome in His peace that passes all understanding. As you practice and repeat this often, my prayer is that it will become a way of living for you, and over time, you will notice that peace has taken up residence within you.

Peace: Redeeming Our Wait

By Chere Wehling

LORD, BE GRACIOUS TO US; WE LONG FOR YOU. BE OUR STRENGTH EVERY MORNING, OUR SALVATION IN TIMES OF DISTRESS.
ISAIAH 33:2, NIV

The scream activated a superpower. I flew up the stairs and threw myself around the corner to see my 13-year-old daughter, Kylie, holding her wrist— blood pooled on our kitchen floor. Making cookies is not a high-risk activity. Maybe a severe burn, but not an injury that requires emergency surgery. She had knocked the glass sugar jar against the granite counter, shattering it. Pulling back in a natural reflex, the shards of glass tore through her wrist.

The adrenaline of the past several hours began to fade. We had raced from our home to one hospital, only to be told we needed to go across town to another hospital that had the required sutures for Kylie's wrist and hand repair. Finally, I sat on the floor in an empty waiting room. Behind the scenes, the surgeon was mirroring the ends of her median nerve, ulnar artery, and multiple tendons–reattaching them in hopes she would regain function and sensation of her hand. With a gentle wave, the fear gave way to peace. My mind calmed from the barrage of questions about her future. In their place came a strange, gentle sense of *enough.* I turned my hurting heart to Jesus. There were no answers, no assurances—only the unmistakable presence of Jesus, steadying me in the waiting. My peace fell as the morning manna did for a fearful ancient Israel–reliable, sustaining, and enough for my need right then.

In a metaphoric sense, we all sit in a waiting room. Our minds keep vigil as we wait for word about what tomorrow will look like. We wonder what will happen when the money runs out, when our bodies fail, or how we keep it all together. Our pain, while real, is exacerbated by our insecurity and concerns for tomorrow. As believers, we wait faithfully, but do we do so peacefully?

Manna: Daily Trust

If there is a group of people who understand insecurity, it's the newly freed Israelites. Rescued from their grueling labor for a brutal regime, they turned to grumbling as their bellies were no longer full. God responds by providing manna every morning. "I have heard the Israelites' complaints. Now tell them, 'In the evening you will have meat to eat, and in the morning you will have all the bread you want. Then you will know that I am the Lord your God" (Exodus 16:12, NLT). They were only to gather what they needed, for any extra bread would spoil. To our Western minds, not being prepared for tomorrow seems inefficient. Why put off what could be done today? However, God was teaching his people to rely on him daily. The scarcity of bread was a mirror revealing their heart posture. They didn't trust God, yet. But in the waiting room of the desert, they could learn.

Peace is like morning manna: you can expect to gather what you need when you need it. It fell in that waiting room just when I needed it. You can't store today's peace for tomorrow. Trusting his faithfulness and his provision protects us from unnecessary fretting today and guards our hearts from tomorrow's chaos.

However, for many believers, our waiting has become a place of anxiety rather than peace—not because we believe God to be unfaithful but because we do not know how to wait well. Our worries for tomorrow, our what-ifs, consume our present. Fixation on our need clouds our awareness of what we do have–Jesus. Ancient Israel also struggled with waiting. There was no food, no market. God didn't eliminate their problem. Each day as they finished their evening meal, they were reminded of the ongoing threat. Their hearts whispered, "There isn't enough." The choice remained: to rest in their knowledge of God's faithfulness and wait for him or grumble about tomorrow.

Waiting for My Day of Distress

In the spring of 2022, my husband had been struggling with his health. What began as minor ailments soon crescendoed into chest pain, weight loss, and severe fatigue. As we sought answers, we were stunned to learn he was in early kidney failure and very anemic. A subsequent urine test revealed Bence Jones proteins, announcing his cancer diagnosis: a bone marrow cancer crowding out healthy cellular growth. His bone marrow was 90% full of Multiple Myeloma. As a nurse and my husband, a physician, we already knew what a Google search would confirm—a two-year prognosis. We were devastated. What followed was a six-month avalanche of drugs, procedures, and grief. The other shoe had dropped. I related to Habakkuk's lament of impending collapse in scripture:

> I heard and my heart pounded, my lips quivered at the sound; decay crept into my bones, and my legs trembled, Yet I will wait patiently for the day of calamity to come on the nation invading us.

> Habakkuk 3:16, NIV

This verse captured the intensity of our anticipatory grief with an additional nod to his bone cancer. Our pain was shaded with the knowledge that his cancer was treatable but incurable. Remission was dangled as healing in reach, but relapse hovered in our periphery. Despite treatment, the cancer lies in wait, learning to evolve and evade the best laid plans- to resurface as a threat. An author and fellow myeloma patient shares it this way, "Living with an incurable disease is like sleeping next to a hibernating bear. For the moment, I knew I was safe, but I knew it was only a matter of time before the bear woke up. And when it did, it would be hungry" (Gluck, ch. 20).

In that space—between reprieve and threat—we found ourselves waiting. Scripture speaks often of waiting on the Lord, repeating the call more than a hundred times. Wherever this rhythm appears, waiting is never passive; it is synonymous with trust. Biblical waiting is the place where our striving ends and our dependence begins.

But our waiting did not feel like trust. It felt like vigilance. Our dread was rooted in harsh realities, and realism became the shield we believed would protect our hearts. Yet, that posture did not prepare us to endure—it numbed us. We insulated ourselves from the very presence we needed to thrive. This was not the waiting scripture invites us into. This was a distorted waiting—a braced, guarded posture. A redeemed wait produces peace because it loosens our grip on what we can control and fixes our gaze on what only God can do.

Warped Waiting

The enemy has a pattern of warping that which God creates. What has been designed for our benefit is twisted, creating counterfeits or distortions. Love, marriage, religion, and the church have all experienced upheaval at the twisting of God's design.

Shortly after my husband, Merlin's, diagnosis, I decided to become an expert on Myeloma and his treatments. I read everything. I was going to protect him from incompetence. I was going to ensure I could ask intelligent questions. My knowledge would give me a template of what to expect. The learning curve was massive, as hematology is hard! Behind a façade of knowing, I reached for control. The irony is, it took a physician, my husband, to remind me, "Chere, sometimes you just need a specialist. Let them handle the Myeloma."

Satan distorts our agency into a need for control by amplifying our fears and keeping us tethered to anxiety. Then he whispers of our scarcity. We don't have enough knowledge. We don't have enough resources. We don't have…. We toil to exert control under the celebrated "I can fix it." Or in my case, "I can manage it." Our fixation agitates, angers, and wounds us. We wait for our day of distress, our eyes fixed on the horizon of loss and pain. The enemy has hijacked our wait. When I surrendered my job as the specialist, relinquishing the task to my husband's doctor, I lightened.

God instituted natural rhythms. Seasons like planting/harvest, Sabbath, and sleep are all designed with a holy wait. The pause, the rest, and the dormancy are all to anticipate what God can do and what He has done. That "wait" is to teach us to trust and to gather hope. The fallow season is the arena where our knowledge of God's goodness goes to work. But instead of the healthy wait that percolates with trust and joy, warped waiting perseverates on fear, and it brings grief. Our season of illness was teaching the difference between what we could influence and what we had to entrust.

Farmers are well acquainted with the rhythms of waiting. They wait for the seasons, seed germination, and weather patterns. Despite the nature of their occupation, farmers don't always wait well. Therefore, they can be challenging as patients. A farmer struggles with the process of healing in the hospital setting. They have things to do. They are anxious that it will all fall apart in their absence. There is a fence that needs fixin', chores to do!

As a nurse in a rural community, I often take care of ranchers and farmers. One particular shift, I had an ornery farmer. After an open colectomy (think 6-inch incision down your abdomen), he kept telling me he was going to leave. With crossed arms, he announces, "I may be 70 years old, but I can outwork any 40-year-old." The subtext- I can do it all, and I am the manliest of the manly. I responded, "Sir, you are a strong man, and what I need you to do now is to man up, sit down, and rest. Your job right now is to sit back and wait. Let your body heal. I know that is hard, but you can do hard things, right?" His wife winked at my boldness, and he blinked when he got the message. There was no further discussion of leaving against medical advice. My point is this-we want to heal well. We desire to thrive and have peace. A redeemed wait can be just what the doctor ordered.

When we wrestle in our hospital bed, inside the wait, we wrestle with the desire to control. The craving for control is the enemy's strategy. Scripture reminds us that we tend to trust in our resources and not God's: "Some trust in chariots and some in horses, but we trust in the name of the Lord our God" (Psalm 20:7, NIV). When we reach for control, we fall out of God's design. "In their hearts humans plan their course, but the Lord establishes their steps" (Proverbs 16:9, NIV). Our desire to control masquerades as worry. Worry is a liturgical act of misplaced trust. It rehearses fear and assigns more power to our circumstances than to our God.

The Wait that Brings Grief

We struggle with two distortions in warped waiting. We carry grief borrowed from tomorrow, imagining every scenario. It is not without good reason. Jesus reminds us, "In this world you will have trouble" (John 16:33, NLT). However, we convince ourselves that our imaginary doom is imminent.

Then there is the anticipatory grief–the kind that we *know* is coming, and it breaks our hearts.

There is no cure, only delay. Your waiting is marked by holding your breath as you adopt the protective posture because your world is unraveling, and if you exhale, the whole lot will land at your feet. The warped wait, the pause between your good day and that which you fear, the impending loss, chips away at stamina and joy. The enemy has taken our insecurity and need and kneaded them into a mangled mess that doesn't resemble trust. This weak substitute promises control; it boasts preparation, but it steals.

I want to discern the difference between rehearsing our fears and holding our sorrow. Loss can not be glossed over. So often, these blur, as they usually occupy the same space. Worry asks for hypervigilance and preparation. Mourning will ask for presence and the space for tears. Our worry can displace our mourning. In my experience, loss, regardless of its scale, can set off a cascade of watchfulness, especially after the first snap of loss, and that can be incredibly disorienting. When fear is talking, its voice can keep us from heart work. We need to mourn. We can, though, separate our healthy lament from fear and worry. Healthy mourning does not crowd out trust: it makes room for it.

More than anything, Christ desires our trust. Jesus would marvel at faith. We see it in the story of the Roman Centurion (Matthew 8:5-13). A Pagan, authoritative man stood in front of Jesus and confessed he wasn't worthy even to have Christ enter his home. Nevertheless, his confidence didn't rest on him -it rested on Christ. He declared that

Jesus only had to command healing for his ailing servant, and restoration would happen. Jesus, in his amazement, responds, " I tell you the truth, I haven't seen faith like this in all Israel" (Matthew 8:10, NLT). "Go back home, because you believed, it has happened" (Matthew 8:13, NLT). In a moment, an ill man is restored; restoration follows trust. Hebrews reminds us that it is impossible to please the Lord without faith. (Hebrews 11:6, NLT) Scripture consistently reframes worship away from *what we do for God* towards *how we trust God.*

To Qāvâ, the Posture of Waiting Well

How often have we been encouraged to *wait on the Lord?* Scripture includes it over one hundred times, so we certainly can trust that to *wait on the Lord* is formative. Unfortunately, what has been impactful has slipped into cliché and is tired. Evaluating the original text and context can be deeply meaningful. Let's look at two words in our understanding of peace:gāal and qāvâ. Here we can gain wisdom.

Our warped waiting needs an intervention or a redemption. The word redemption in Hebrew is Gāal. At its heart, gāal is a relational saving. Its rescue is not by a stranger but by one who is bound by covenant love. To gāal our wait, we need to refocus it on our redeemer rather than on our circumstances or our resources. This posture of trust will help us with our need for peace. "Therefore, say to the people of Israel: 'I am the Lord. I will free you from your oppression and will rescue you from your slavery in Egypt. I will redeem (gāal) you with a powerful arm and great acts of judgment" (Exodus 6:6, NLT).

In most cases, when reading scripture, the translation of "wait" comes from the Hebrew word qāvâ. In Hebrew, most words have both literal and figurative meanings. These two perspectives stood out to me.

qāvâ (wait)

> The figurative definition -waiting with anticipation, to eagerly look forward
>
> The literal definition- To bind up, collect, intertwine, twist, stretch, tension of enduring

We can infer, with these definitions fresh in our minds, that waiting is not something to endure or survive. The invitation to wait on the Lord is relational. Waiting on the Lord is not idle–it is walking with Him. We can now gāʾal (redeem) our wait in three ways.

Anticipation: Seek to Know God

It's been almost four years since Merlin's diagnosis. We still don't know the future. His quarterly oncology visits are a frequent reminder that our lives are especially fragile. But yet, Jesus has shown up. The ability to have peace and joy even when there doesn't seem to be enough time, enough health, can only be explained by clinging to the abundance that remains in Jesus. David writes in Psalms, "It was good for me that I'm afflicted so that I may learn your decrees (Psalm 119:71, NIV). Suffering has the quiet privilege of re-fining our theology. We both thought we knew a great deal about faith. Over time, our pursuit of faith had become a storehouse of doctrine. But doctrine doesn't help you sleep at night. When a spiritual famine comes, doctrine cannot sustain you. Our posture shifted from acquiring knowledge to seeking presence and to knowing God. Faith became less about what we could explain and more about whom we could trust.

To qāvâ on the Lord is a natural rhythm that lends itself to focus on who God is. The Roman Centurion displayed his confidence in Christ's ability, and that posture is a posture of waiting well. Our present reality is not the bigger picture. In our focus on God's character, we make room for God to move. Not that God needs our consent, but we have a mental buffer that enables us to see possibilities. Instead of asking why, we can expectantly ask how God will work. The mystery isn't whether he will show up. The mystery is how He redeems this circumstance (Romans 8:28).

If knowing God is where the power lies, how we read scripture should change. Author Skye Jethani shares it this way. " When the Bible is primarily seen as the depository of divine principles for life, it fundamentally changes the way we engage God and His Word. Rather than a vehicle for knowing God and fostering our communion with him, we search the scriptures for applicable principles that we may employ to control our world and life (Jethani, 51). There, nestled in fragile pages, are stories of people like you and me revealing God's plan of redemption, his character, and his pursuit of us. Reflecting on God's heart will prime you to see him at work in your future.

Binding Up, Collecting: Choosing to Pray

During Kylie's hand injury, as I sat in the waiting room, exhaustion set in. My mind recounted the image of finding her holding her wrist. I had run for a towel and applied pressure. Then things got woozy, and I did the only thing I could think of: I yelled for my husband. When he arrived, he had two patients. My face was as white as a sheet, and Kylie was bleeding out. He placed both of us on the floor and got to work binding Kylie's wrist. Can you imagine what would have happened if I had ignored the physician in the house? Yet so often in our daily lives, we try to manage as a woozy patient ourselves, overwhelmed with the scene in front of us. The alarm system is activated, and then we try to muddle through on our own strength.

Just as I needed help in that moment, so often in life we find ourselves overwhelmed and trying to manage alone–ignoring the One who is ever-present to intervene. Jesus says we would have trouble in this world. We are told to be alert. We have picked up that charge and do that very well. Often primed for threats, we are on high alert most of the time. So much so, we miss the rest of the imperative. Stay alert **and** pray (Matthew 26:41, Mark 14:38, Luke 21:36)! Our alertness is not meant to keep our nervous system teetering on the edge. Instead, our alertness to threat is to *wait on the Lord*. We are to *collect* ourselves and *bind* our fears up in Jesus. Peter reminds us we are to be alert and sober-minded **for** prayer. (1 Peter 4:7) Collect ourselves, ask for help, and remember Jesus's invitation: Come to me. (Matthew 11:28)

"Stay alert, so you can pray" is an invitation to intimacy. This perspective moves our prayers past the presentation of needs to an awareness of God's presence. Our prayers center us on the promise that he draws near to the broken-hearted.

(Psalm 34:18) Talking to God is where he promises to *bind* up our wounds and our fears. "He heals the brokenhearted and bandages their wounds"(Psalm 147:4, Isaiah 30:26).

Twist and stretch: Build something new, stronger

Qāvâ is more than passive waiting; it is a waiting under tension. This wait is to twist and stretch, to give something a new shape, one that is stronger. It's the tension that brings strength over time, revealing an active inner work. It is the same reality that gives us strong bodies. Repeated tension brings strength. Qāvâ stretches the heart and mind, reshaping them over time. We can trust this process, not wither under it.

Kylie's hand recovery provides a vivid example of this kind of tension. As a teenager, you are learning who you are and seeking ways to express it. Music was an essential part of what it meant to be "Kylie". Her hand injury threatened her love of cello, French horn, and piano. It was a painful physical recovery as well. Rehab was aimed at reducing pain sensitization caused by overactive nerves and tendons that were trying to adhere to and pull on the scar tissue.

Pain is meant to signal danger, to urge protection, but Kylie's healing wrist and hand had become *too* sensitive. Her brain no longer distinguished between threat and safety. The overactive pain receptors were firing inappropriately, leading to increased pain. To recover function, she would take a rough-bristled brush and deliberately move it across the scar—again and again—forcing sensation to retrain her brain. The therapy was not about toughening the skin, but about **re-educating trust**. With each careful pass of the brush, her nerves and brain were taught a new truth: this sensation was not a threat. She was safe.

Qāvâ is the brushstroke that reminds our tender hearts that we are safe. That, despite our insecurity, regardless of our broken bodies reacting with fear, the God of heaven is speaking over us-you're safe, you have enough. I'm here. It is difficult to enter into this divine therapy. We want to avoid the pain; we want to do our own therapy. Our waiting on him resets our minds, creating something better. We can thrive even with our scars.

Jesus came alongside Kylie, revealing that the pain and loss of her hand for a season could help her grow. She wrote songs, sang more, and learned to play the trumpet because it didn't require her damaged left hand. She blossomed. She discovered that Jesus was her friend, and that relationship motivated the very work that rehabilitated her hand to full function. Jesus inspired her with music, and as she sat at the piano with a wounded heart and hand, she played. Her fingers relearning and moving at the impulse of love. Ten years later, she is on her way to medical school, with a tenderness for those who need healing, an awe at how the body can heal, and a confidence that Jesus walks with her. What her mama feared would strip her future, Jesus multiplied into abundance.

Our qāvâ builds something in us that enables us to trust more and more. I think that is why Jesus says if you have faith (trust) the size of a mustard seed, you can move a mountain. From little, much can grow (Matthew 17:20, Luke 17:6). The seed is stretched under tension, twisted by challenge, and over time, it grows stronger. What was once fragile or damaged develops the strength to hold you steady even in a mountainous crisis.

Encouragement for the Enduring: Tension of Waiting

Friends, I know waiting on the Lord is not easy. However, I want to encourage you that a qāvâ grounded in a relationship with Christ will help you hang on. We see this in a powerful exchange in John 6. The story kicks off where Jesus and the disciples are mobbed. Jesus has just fed the 5000, and the people wanted more miracles. In fact, Jesus had to flee earlier because they wanted to make him King. They witnessed His power and wanted to use Jesus to solve their political and economic problems. (John 6:15). They beg Jesus to display his power again. But he doesn't. Instead, he promises a deeper provision, one that transforms the heart. The people go on to demand, "Give us manna." But Jesus reminds them that their manna doesn't save them from death. He invites a swapping of physical bread for spiritual bread, promising it will satisfy.

But we want miracles. We plead for our circumstances to change. I pray for a Myeloma cure, but only get a delay. I pray for drugs with no side effects. I pray for things to be easier. We want confirmation of the Divine. But Jesus doesn't use his power like that. The mob, disgusted by Jesus's refusal, starts to leave. The disciples read the room and echo the sentiment. "This is very hard to understand. How can anyone accept it?" (John 6:60, NLT). You mean to tell us, Jesus, you have all this power, and sometimes you won't use it? A hard truth indeed.

Then Jesus turns to his friends, his disciples, and poses a heartbreaking question, "Will you leave too?" Peter, in one of my favorite moments in scripture, responds, "Lord, to whom shall we go? You have the words of eternal life?" (John 6:68, NIV). Peter, in relationship with Jesus, had seen too much. He knew better. Though confused and unsure of Jesus' plan, he didn't want to be separated from Christ.

When developing a posture of trust, we can be tempted to think that our confidence in Jesus' abilities will somehow manifest what we want. We want healing, relief, and justice, but we know all too well we don't always get them this side of heaven. However, Jesus promises something better. Peter's answer says this: intimacy with Jesus will give you enough endurance to hang on, and Jesus promises it will satisfy. "Peace I leave with you; my peace I give to you. I do not give to you as the world gives. Don't let your heart be troubled or fearful (John 14: 27, NIV).

Jesus referring to himself as the Bread of Life in John 6, among the shadow of unresolved questions and unused power, is no accident. It is meant to connect us to a powerful image of something beyond scarcity. To say you are at peace is to say you have **enough**, you have Jesus. Jesus is always enough- He is our manna. "I am the bread of life (John 6:35, NIV). "For the bread of God is the one who comes down from heaven and gives life to the world (John 6:33, NIV). Manna falling from heaven pointed to the reality of Jesus's presence. His presence is what satisfies, what brings peace. He is available daily, and trying to store that which is relational is temporary at best. Our trust in Jesus is meant to be lived out daily. We can wait with qāvâ, receiving him, or with worry, grasping at control–but only trust ensures that we are fed, held, and aware of his sustaining presence.

What is your next right thing?

After Merlin's cancer diagnosis, we felt overwhelmed with all the decisions that needed to be made. As planners, we felt disoriented because we couldn't discern the future. We just didn't have enough information. Should he keep working? What should we do about our business? Should we downsize? Was his prognosis really two years? That question alone made everything seem urgent.

Qāvâ for us looked like doing the next right thing; a cliche, yes, but rooted in scripture. "Give your entire attention to what God is doing right now, and don't get worked up about what may or may not happen tomorrow. God will help you deal with whatever hard things come up when the time comes" (Matthew 6:34, The Message). This verse brings us back to the importance of accepting our provision, manna for today. By focusing on the present, we learned to surrender and to look for Jesus there.

Recently, the power of surrender hit home. I received my nursing assignment for the day, which included a patient with Myeloma who was dying–the same cancer my husband had. This gentleman had tried every available treatment, and they no longer worked. My first instinct was: *I can't do this. I don't want to see this.* This poor man was failing in front of us.

However, assignments were made, and I didn't want to disrupt my peers. I prayed, *Lord, I'm not sure I can do this– it hurts way too much.* Quietly, the Lord whispered to my heart, *You can because I'm here, and you are the best person for the job.*

What? Me–why? Because I knew and understood this family's story. I knew the enemy and understood the battle. So I served him, washed his body, and tended his needs as if he were my own husband.

Friends, there is an image of Jesus in Isaiah that I love: "So the Lord must wait for you to come to him so he can show you his love and compassion. For the Lord is a faithful God. Blessed are those who wait for his help (Isaiah 30:18, NLT). Do you see it? Jesus is waiting for you to wait on him. If my knowledge of my patient made me the best nurse, how much more is Jesus the best redeemer for us? He also knows the battle, the enemy, and we are already his. There is no pain that he hasn't himself visited. What are we waiting for?

If you remember, to redeem or Gā'al is to rescue–to return that which has been stolen back into the safety of the family. The enemy has stolen our wait by infusing it with worry, scarcity, and control. Thereby divorcing our qāvâ from Jesus' companionship as a weak platitude. Waiting well involves reclaiming the purpose of our wait-to sit with Jesus. Are you able to identify where your wait has been hijacked? Can you point to feelings of dread, insecurity, and anger? Do you ruminate on the what-ifs, and does that add to your distress? " Developing a practice of qāvâ reorients your mind to his presence over your problem.

When a feeling of impending doom shows up, instead of dwelling on the unknown and strategizing, choose to pray. Consider David's prayer asking God to enlighten him,

"Show me the wonders of your great love, you who save by your right hand those who take refuge in you from their foes" (Psalm 17:7, NIV).

Sometimes those prayers seem unanswered, and God appears quiet. This can be discouraging. However, because qāvâ reorients our hearts towards the goodness of God, his abundant promises to be with us, we can rest in the knowledge that the mind and heart are undergoing a transformation. The wait, the dormancy, while yoked to Jesus, is actually producing an inner work that will make you stronger. Each time you turn over your fears and hurts to Jesus, you are twisting and binding your wait, your trust, into something new, something stronger.

Qāvâ is the rhythm of a heart that facilitates intimacy with God. Who has God unveiled himself to be to you? What can you read today that reinforces God's heart as your redeemer, both merciful and kind? Choosing trust over control, meditating on God's character, and remembering to pray are all spiritual practices of a heart that sows God's faithfulness and harvests peace. Where can you find satisfaction in not knowing the future because you know Jesus?

Your next right thing is to choose Jesus. This wait, when redeemed and restored from what the enemy snatched, not only frees you from the bondage of dread–it restores you, filling you with peace; Jesus's presence. Peace isn't found in solutions or resolutions. Peace is found in a promise, for Jesus and peace are synonymous: " You will keep in perfect peace all who trust in you, all whose thoughts are fixed on you (Isaiah 26:3, NLT)! Precious Lord Jesus, take my hand.

Chapter 8

Listening: His Voice Above the Noise

By Becky Sims

> BE STILL, AND KNOW THAT I AM GOD. I WILL BE EXALTED
> AMONG THE NATIONS, I WILL BE EXALTED IN THE EARTH!
> PSALM 46:10, NKJV

One day, while I was in college, I sat in my car waiting over an hour for an empty parking spot. I used this time to pray. My high school classmate, Jami, came to mind. I'd seen her a few times around campus, but we didn't have any classes together. She had lost two family members during our senior year. I asked, "Lord, when possible, I'd really like to see Jami again. She's had a difficult time lately, and I just want to know that she's okay. Also, I could really use a parking spot. I'm late for class." As I opened my eyes and looked ahead, I saw Jami walking toward me! I rolled down my window, and we chatted briefly.

Amazingly, Jami was heading to her car and said I could have her parking spot! Normally, there would be many cars waiting for spots, but this time, there was no one else around. I backed my car down the long aisle, across a street, and to the far end of the lot. Once parked, I ran all the way to class laughing while thanking God for His sense of humor!

The Lord is eager to connect with us. He created us to be in relationship with Him. We can start by spending time in our Bibles. His Word is our instruction book and the best way for us to learn more about Him, His Son Jesus, and the Holy Spirit. It is full of His truths and teachings on how to live our lives for Him. David said in Psalm 119:105 (NKJV). "Your word is a lamp to my feet And a light to my path." God's Word is the primary way He communicates with us.

Hebrews 4:12 (NKJV) states, "For the word of God is living and powerful, and sharper than any two-edged sword, piercing even to the division of soul and spirit, and of joints and marrow, and is a discerner of the thoughts and intents of the heart." And in 2 Timothy 3:16-17 (NKJV), we're reminded that, "All Scripture is given by inspiration of God, and is profitable for doctrine, for reproof, for correction, for instruction in righteousness, that the man of God may be complete, thoroughly equipped for every good work." The more we are in His Word, the easier it will be to recognize His voice.

At times, we can "hear" or sense God's presence, and He allows us to see Him in action right away, just like He did for me on that day. But more often, His voice is softer and we "hear" Him in our hearts and minds as we sit quietly, in prayer and praise, or peaceful reflection.

God sent the Holy Spirit to live inside each of His children. "Do you not know that you are the temple of God and that the Spirit of God dwells in you?" (1 Corinthians 3:16, NKJV). It's through the Holy Spirit that we communicate our prayers, even when we're unable to express them in words. "Likewise, the Spirit also helps in our weaknesses. For we do not know what we should pray for as we ought, but the Spirit Himself makes intercession for us with groanings which cannot be uttered" (Romans 8:26, NKJV).

It's also the Spirit Who leads us into truth. "But the Helper, the Holy Spirit, whom the Father will send in My name, He will teach you all things, and bring to your remembrance all things that I said to you" (John 14:26, NKJV).

As the Holy Spirit leads us, we desire to do all things for Him, but we know we can't do everything. Looking around us, we see an abundance of needs. There are endless areas where we could get involved, and our minds race with possibilities. Yet, our schedules may already be full. We long to move forward, but this struggle holds us back. We ask the Lord to guide our steps so that we can serve a need with confidence.

There are also times when we're focused on life's difficulties, on the things we can't control. In those moments, our peace is lost. Our energy is drained. Our courage is gone. Even then, we can ask the Lord for His guidance, reminding ourselves that He lovingly wants what's best for us. We can share our burdens and ask Him to provide patience and understanding while we wait and pray. "For your Father knows the things you have need of before you ask Him" (Matthew 6:8b, NKJV). In fact, God says, "For I know the plans I have for you, declares the Lord, plans for welfare and not for evil, to give you a future and a hope" (Jeremiah 29:11, ESV).

Simple statements of faith encourage us to see that there are blessings even in the tough times…

"Thank You, Lord, for another day!"
"Thank You for those who surround me with love."
"I am a child of God."
"With the Lord's help, I will get through this difficulty."

As our hearts and minds focus on God's gifts of patience and compassion, we will sense His help and closeness and find the ability to persevere in His peace. I experienced His peace during a hospitalization with my first pregnancy. I had a high leak in my amniotic fluid, and I was placed on strict bed rest and told that if I got up, it could cause serious complications for my baby. I had to give up doing anything for myself and rely on others for that time. My husband brought in a magnet from our nursery and hung it high on the door frame. It was an image of Noah's Ark with the words, "God keeps His promises."

My relationship with the Lord and all of the experiences that He had already brought me through allowed me to have the faith that He would continue to help me through this, too. I lived out the verse, "Be anxious for nothing, but in everything by prayer and supplication, with thanksgiving, let your requests be made known to God; and the peace of God, which surpasses all understanding, will guard your hearts and minds through Christ Jesus" (Philippians 4:6-7, NKJV). The Lord sustained me through that week, the next

9 weeks that I spent on bed rest at home, and all the days that have followed as I have raised my family.

These experiences and many others have shown me the importance of connecting with the Lord throughout our days. I have seen that when we **pray for discernment**, **actively listen**, and **walk in wisdom**, we are able to move closer to the Lord and humbly follow His lead. Let's take a closer look at each of these areas.

Pray for Discernment:

"Because He has inclined His ear to me, therefore I will call upon Him as long as I live."

Psalm 116:2, NKJV

Discernment is needed when we're seeking to understand which direction to go. God expects us to "cry out for discernment" (Proverbs 2:3, NKJV) and ask for wisdom. "If any of you lacks wisdom, let him ask of God, who gives to all liberally and without reproach, and it will be given to him" (James 1:5, NKJV).

In our lives, we will encounter many situations that require repeated prayer and deep focus for discernment. God is our light, and He illuminates the path for us. It may just be the one next step we are to take in faith. But He promises to be with us, to guide and order our lives. As we navigate each day, we need His strength and direction. That's why we must never stop praying for Him to lead us forward on the narrow path.

Let's seek God and draw closer to Him. We can give Him our daily struggles, desires, sorrows, and triumphs. We can share our gratitude for Him and rest in His presence. Whether our day is filled with minor difficulties or major detours, seeking discernment through prayer will help us to rest in His loving peace. He will support and direct us, promising to reward us for our faithfulness.

Here are three steps to help us find peace as we pray for discernment:

1. Share and Surrender.

   Reach out to the Lord. Share your questions and concerns with Him and place them in His hands. Acknowledge Him as your Heavenly Father and the One you put your trust in. Spend a moment praising Him for what He has already done in your life.

2. Calm Your Heart and Mind.

   Choose an activity that helps to calm your body and slow your pace. Deep breathing and focused repetition of a favorite Bible verse are two great options. When we take the time to focus on God's Word and slow our pace, we're less distracted by the world.

   In the foreword of *24/6: A Prescription for a Healthier, Happier Life* by Matthew Sleeth, MD, Eugene Peterson shares a unique way to use Scripture to focus on the truth of the Lord. "And here is a meditative practice that I find attractive. Until now, I had never come across subtracting one word at a time from Psalm 46:10 to help me come to rest. 'Be still and know that I am God'" (p. ix). The idea is to remove the last word each time you silently repeat the verse, inhaling for the first four words, and exhaling for the last four, maintaining this rhythm even after the words are gone.

I have used this practice to relax during the difficult moments in my day and to help me fall asleep at night. Repeating the Bible truths in this way helps me center my heart on the Lord's unfailing love and gain a quiet closeness which enables me to feel His presence. Take some time to experiment with different activities to find what works best for you.

3. Ask for a Teachable Heart that will Discern His Voice.

    Share your requests with the Lord and rely on Him. Ask IIim to make you willing to learn, change, and grow for whatever He has planned for you. Thank Him for listening and let Him know you will keep asking, but will humbly wait for Him to answer in His timing.

Actively Listen:

"My sheep hear My voice, and I know them, and they follow Me." John 10:27, NKJV

I love the "lightbulb moments" sent by the Lord!

During my college of education coursework, I had the opportunity to choose between student teaching for only the fall quarter or remaining in a classroom for a full school year. I would either graduate sooner or have more experience with a master teacher before heading out on my own.

This was a big decision for me, and as usual, I had been sharing it with the Lord in prayer and mulling it over in my mind for some time. One evening, as I was cleaning out the microwave after closing at my fast food job, I was thinking through both scenarios, quietly waiting for the "right" answer to pop into my head. Then, as if a bright light switched on before my eyes, the answer was clear! I was to stay for the full year! I knew this was clearly God's plan for me. I would gain experience in every classroom activity. I could participate with these students for an extended period of time, first as a student teacher, and then as a lead teacher. This increased the possibility of being hired by the school system. I even earned a small stipend and some retirement benefits.

God promises that He has a direction for our lives. He reveals the next step of the plan in His timing, sometimes in a lightbulb moment and other times gradually and after lots of waiting, but always at just the right time. We can thank the Lord for sending us both the quiet answers and the lightbulb moments!

Here are three steps to enhance our ability to hear the Lord's voice:

1. Open Your Ears.

   Practice listening daily for His voice. Step away from the distractions and slow your pace on purpose. Ask Him to speak to you. Sitting in the stillness and calming quiet will allow you to focus your attention on the Lord and His gentle nudgings.

2. Listen with Expectation.

   Remain aware of the Lord's presence and quietly listen without pressure. Don't strain to "hear something." God often speaks as we are moving through our activities.

3. Seek Godly Counsel.

    Wise Christian friends and confidants can help confirm what is best in our current situations. Working with those we trust helps to strengthen our faith. We're better able to discern in community.

As we apply these three concepts, the answers may come slowly, or they may come like lightbulb moments. When we're at peace, with a sense of inner stillness, we can wait patiently and move forward with the guidance He provides. We can hear His voice above the noise and live fully connected to Him. We can continue to pray with faith, listen with confidence, and walk in wisdom.

Walk in Wisdom:

My son, if you receive my words,
    And treasure my commands within you,
So that you incline your ear to wisdom,
    And apply your heart to understanding;

Yes, if you cry out for discernment,
    And lift up your voice for understanding,
If you seek her as silver,
    And search for her as for hidden treasures;
Then you will understand the fear of the LORD,
    And find the knowledge of God.

Proverbs 2:1-5, NKJV

By staying close to the Lord and asking for His guidance for all of our needs and plans, we'll gain the confidence to do whatever He asks. This is a continual practice of reaching out to Him, listening, and applying what we have been given. He will remain with each of us, enabling us to accomplish His plans in His way and in His time.

In high school, I told my best friend that I liked to pray as I walked the halls in between my classes. The halls were packed with people hurrying to their lockers or gathering together for quick conversations. But I remained calm. Those few minutes with the Lord gave me the strength and confidence to keep moving through my day. And my friend told me she purposefully wouldn't say anything to me so she wouldn't interrupt my prayer time!

We can all hear the Lord speak into our hearts, though it takes consistent and intentional time to grow in our awareness. God will help us discern where we are being called. He'll also show us what we're not called to do at this time. And even when we are equipped for a role, it might not be ours to fill right now. He may have something we're better suited for coming our way.

Life is full of challenges and opportunities for us to navigate. When we rely on the Lord and invite Him into our hearts consistently, we'll find our trust in Him gives us the confidence to do what He has called us to do with His help.

Here are three steps to help us walk in the Lord's wisdom:

1. Trust God's Timing.

    The Lord has a different sense of timing. The earth is bound by chronology, with moments passing by the minutes, hours, days, and years. But the Lord can see and be everywhere at once. He knows everything from the beginning to the end of time.

"But, beloved, do not forget this one thing, that with the Lord one day is as a thousand years, and a thousand years as one day" (2 Peter 3:8, NKJV). We can trust that His timing is best.

At times, this means waiting. "Wait on the Lord; Be of good courage, And He shall strengthen your heart; Wait, I say, on the Lord!" (Psalm 27:14, NKJV) This may mean staying where you are until He tells you to move, or spending more time in prayerful consideration before taking the next step. It could also mean waiting for the needed training, support, or finances. The Lord has a reason when He makes us wait. And when the time comes for action, the reward will be so much sweeter.

2. Prepare for the Project.

For which of you, intending to build a tower, does not sit down first and count the cost, whether he has enough to finish it—lest, after he has laid the foundation, and is not able to finish, all who see it begin to mock him, saying, 'This man began to build and was not able to finish'?

Luke 14:28-30, NKJV

My husband and I have built two homes together. Both times, we prepared by reviewing the floor plans, touring the homes we were considering, choosing the specific lot, and deciding which custom options would make the home uniquely ours. We considered our budget and allocated funds accordingly for the items.

As we prepare for any project, we examine what is needed to take it through to completion. We can gather the items, funding, and resources, and allocate the time.

3. Apply What You've Learned.

"But be doers of the word, and not hearers only, deceiving yourselves." James 1:22, NKJV

In His timing, we'll feel the nudge and know it's aligned with the character of our Father and His Son, Jesus. It will also be aligned with the Bible, because God never contradicts Himself. We can then move forward in the peace He provides.

Since we have also prepared for the project, we will have what is needed to take the next steps in confidence. We can follow through on what He is calling us to do. Though the tasks may not be easy, the Lord will help us through.

Continuous Connection:

"Rejoicing in hope, patient in tribulation, continuing steadfastly in prayer." Romans 12:12, NKJV

Stay connected to the Lord at all times. Check in when things are going great, when they're tough, and any time in between. He's always with us, working behind the scenes. We are to call on Him, be still and listen, and then move in positive ways while we wait for His guidance. We can continue to follow this process on repeat.

When we hear the Lord's voice above the noise of this world, we'll find peace.

These things I have spoken to you, that in Me you may have peace. In the world you will have tribulation; but be of good cheer, I have overcome the world.

John 16:33, NKJV

Our patience can continue to grow even in the midst of trials. God often uses these difficulties to refine us. As we focus on growing closer to Him in these times, we can be encouraged by remembering all of the past situations He has brought us through.

Faith allows us to trust and pray to our Father, even though we can't see Him, and to believe He loves us and will help us through whatever we encounter. God will be there, cheering us on and catching us when we fall. He will send us the helpers and insights we need to continue moving through life.

Let's aim to become more present in His peace and see what this fruit of the Spirit brings into our lives and the lives of those we touch.

My Soul Be Still

Often, the tasks on our to-do lists keep us moving, and we don't take time to sit with the Lord. One evening, while getting ready to wash the dishes, I felt the urge to sit and listen to what He had for me. I jotted this poem as I rested with Him.

My soul be still
to hear God's will.
Be not full of struggle
but rest fully in His Love.

Hope in His promises.
Have faith in His Word.
His truths are sure.
With Him I can endure.

There is nothing my God cannot do.
Every morning His mercies are new.
He's with me every day,
always showing me the Way.
He's lovingly calling me back to Him.

I cannot earn His Love.
It was freely given from above.
God sent His Son to save my soul,
so eternity with Him is possible.
It's promised to me if I believe.

To hear God's will,
my soul be still.

After my quiet time with Him, I went back to the dishes with my heart refreshed and ready for my evening plans.

Listening to the Lord and following Him means being open and aware of His presence. He is always near. There will be seasons when we hear Him more than others. But we can make space for Him when we sit quietly and meditate on His Word, or listen with our minds open to what He has for us. These times alone with Him give us peace and hope, allowing us to continue on with the work He has given us.

PRAYER: *Dear Lord, thank You for Your still small voice and the reminder to spend time with You. Your presence in our lives brings us comfort, hope, guidance, and peace. Please continue to call us to You and help us stay connected with You at all times. In Christ's name, Amen.*

Chapter 9

Peaceful Presence:
Pursuing Silence

By Alana Deutschmann

"THE LORD IS IN HIS HOLY TEMPLE; LET ALL THE EARTH BE SILENT BEFORE HIM." HABAKKUK 2:20, NIV

It was another typical evening bedtime routine. I climbed up the ladder to lie next to my 9-year-old daughter in her loft bed as it was time to listen to her read a couple of pages in a chapter book. A handful of minutes later, I hear, "What do you think she's going to do, Mom?" Because I didn't have an answer, again I hear, "Mom?" In those few moments of her asking the question, I realized I hadn't actually listened to a word that she just read. Sure, I may have been physically present, but my mind was a mile away. I was going over my still-to-be-done list that evening, replaying a conversation with a friend from the day before, fretting about that appointment tomorrow, and therefore I embarrassingly had to say, I'm so sorry, honey, but I zoned out, so I don't know what she's going to do."

"Mo—om."

" I know, I know, I'm sorry. I got distracted, but I'll pay better attention next time."

I wish that I could tell you that this was a rare occurrence, but struggling to focus and be present had been going on for far too long. Can you relate?

I would venture to say that most of us have been guilty of or experienced this, maybe with a child, parent, friend, spouse, co-worker, coach, or boss. But we usually just blame our schedules or our sleep. Sometimes we even give a pass to the person because, hey, we've all done it, right? Of course, there is grace for us to give ourselves and others, but I was growing more frustrated, restless, and simply tired of a disengaged existence, letting life happen *to* me.

During a wilderness season of chronic physical health issues years prior to that evening, my life had slowed to a pace of existing to take care of my little family. I remember starting to take short drives with the radio off and cooking a meal without listening to anything. While pushing my daughter in her stroller around the zoo, I started noticing not just the animals, of course, but the flowers blooming along the path, the changing colors of the trees, the shimmer of the sun reflecting off the lake, the bold white clouds that looked like marshmallows clumped together on top of hot chocolate. Scripture was coming to mind more frequently as I recalled Jesus' words about considering how the lilies don't toil but grow, and how if He cares for even the sparrows, why would He not care for me, His beloved child? (Matthew 6:26, ESV)

I couldn't have described what was happening at the time, but through spontaneous periods of silence, I was contemplating the mystery, wonder, and beauty of being alive.

There is a lot to say about silence, and yes, I fully acknowledge the irony in that, but I want to guide us to see that intentionally pursuing silence helps us to be better present with God, ourselves, and others.

Depending on your Christian tradition or upbringing, you may or may not be familiar with silence as a spiritual discipline or practice; in fact, it may have made you recoil a little or feel uncomfortable to the point that you're already writing me off as a new age pagan mystic. Therefore, I want to start by clarifying what silence is NOT.

The focus on silence is not about entirely emptying the mind.

One of the biggest differences between Christian meditation and Eastern traditions is mindFULLness versus mindLESSness. We seek to fill our minds with the Truth of the Scriptures and yield to the Holy Spirit's presence within our bodily temples.

We're not magnifying ourselves or our metaphorical storms, but rather elevating Christ's finished work and His promises to us.

Silence is not staying quiet or ignoring when injustice or abuse is happening. Certainly not everything requires our response, opinion, or action; therefore, wisdom and discernment are necessary for the *when* and *how* of speaking up and taking action, otherwise we risk getting stuck in complicity or apathy.

After I was already practicing periods of silence, I learned about three kinds of noise- auditory, informational, and internal, which gave me a helpful framework from which to inventory the level of noise in my life. I didn't want to keep normalizing distraction, and I certainly wanted to be able to better connect with my daughter about what she was reading to me.

Before we go any further, let's define each of them.

Auditory noise is a compilation of mechanical, digital, and human noise. Man-made sounds, nature, people's voices-a.k.a "the modern world." Examples include phone calls and notifications, engine revving vehicles, ambulance and fire truck sirens, construction sites, helicopters, barking dogs, honking geese, wind gusts, thunderstorms, cicadas and bullfrogs, machines in workplaces and homes, forklifts, printers, lawn mowers, and vacuums. Did you know that movie theater noise has increased since the 1980's and 90s? Typical human conversations are in the 60-70 decibel range, while 85 is the standard considered safe for watching a 2-3 hour movie in a theater; however, studies have found films ranging from 74-104 decibels, including some children's movies. Without any form of protection, damage can occur within 15 minutes or when 100-104+ decibels are reached.(1)

When I refer to Informational noise, this is about cutting down the never-ending onslaught of content we are bombarded by on a daily basis. From newspapers and magazines (printed or online) to video, audio, e-mails, and social media. While the amount of information continues to increase over time, our capacity to handle or process it does not.

Lastly, we come to Internal noise. This may very well be the hardest part to quiet, and it sounds like positive and negative repetitive thoughts, beliefs, and opinions about myself and others, basic tasks and scheduling, worry, fear, doubt, hopes and dreams, the past, and the future. There is a difference between suppressing and quieting, though. Oftentimes, we don't even know how loud our internal chatter actually is because we don't take breaks from the informational or external noise.

Silence as Presence with God

I believe silence increases a healthy fear of God, the kind where you are afraid to be away from Him. Think about some of the best places you've visited in creation- standing on the shoreline of a pristine lake or the sandy beach of an ocean, the top of a mountain, Niagara Falls, the Grand Canyon, or looking up at the gigantic Redwood Trees. Places that can take your breath and words away. One doesn't figure out what the practical lesson is in those moments because the natural, appropriate response is awe and worship of the Creator. In this way, I have practiced quieting the informational and internal noise to tune into the auditory sounds of Nature.

Silence is this opening, leveling, swelling of the presence of God within and all around me.

If my very lifestyle is worship and He is truly omnipresent, I can commune with Him anywhere and anytime, but I have found that the more I seek to minimize noisy stimuli, the better I can hear Him.

There is an overwhelming amount of Christian/Biblical content out there and I am guilty of consuming 15 different subjects at one time trying to digest it all or keep up with all of the different topics of conversation happening online or in real life instead of seeking the Lord's guidance on which area to spend more time on this particular day, week, or season.

Many of us talk *at* God, rather than with Him, often forgetting the listening part. What if, at first, we tried quieting all the things we want to say to Him, all the internal chatter, and just practiced being delighted in by our Heavenly Father, receiving His love for us as His dear children?

The more I learned about neuroscience, the more in awe I was of God as master Creator and designer of this world and my body. He has made a way for us to experience real shalom (wholeness) even during this "already-but-not-yet" time frame we currently live in. Reverence induced humility and silence was the catalyst. I recognize who He is and who I am not. I am a finite creature, wholly dependent on the Everlasting King. He is the Shepherd, and I am the sheep. He is the potter, and I am the clay. In silence, I experience the *both/and* nature of my smallness and my significance. I recognize who I am because of who He is and what He has done. I am a fickle human being made of the dust of the ground, yet chosen, unconditionally loved, and redeemed by the blood of Jesus. Because He is worthy, I am worthy. And this Holy God wants a relationship with you and me. He wants to fill us with His Spirit and take on His easy yoke to work out our salvation and grow in Christlikeness. He wants to co-labor with us to see the gospel being proclaimed and the kingdom expanding in all the nations. What a marvelous gift!

Silence as Presence with Myself

The more I practiced times of silencing outer noise - conversation, music, podcasts, entertainment, technology in general- the more I was able to pay attention to my inner noise and quickly learned that quiet does not automatically equal peace because trauma can be loud. Regret can be loud. Betrayal can be loud. The inner critic can be loud. Emotions can be loud. The imposter syndrome can be loud. Symptoms can be loud. Expectations can be loud. On top of this, kids can be loud. The washing machine can be loud. The calendar can be loud, and the neighbors can be loud, so there are still other noises to contend with at the same time.

However, paying attention to the aforementioned list led to awareness, and from that place, I became curious about my thoughts, beliefs, and emotions without judgment. I stopped bullying myself into thinking better and recognized how I was self-sabotaging by continuing to perpetuate an inner narrative of "not good enough." I can't do enough or be enough for my family, friends, the church, or the world. I believed that I was "too much" to handle with all of my medical complexities and made up stories in my mind about what others must think of me and my situation. My coping mechanisms of choice were binging cheesy television shows and distracting myself by scrolling through YouTube or other social media sites. When I caught myself exhibiting any of these thoughts or behaviors, I worked on being compassionately firm in how I coached myself to receive His Truths and renew my mind. Romans 8:6, ESV says, "For to set the mind on the flesh is death, but to set the mind on the spirit is life and peace." It seems much easier to ruminate and dwell on the past, or to become anxious about the future, because it has become familiar or even habitual. Taking every thought captive enables us to live in the present moment, which, in turn, contributes to change and growth. When we're thinking about what is "true, honorable, just, pure, lovely, and commendable," we give ourselves a much better chance at speaking wisely when we do talk, since it is out of the overflow of the heart that the mouth speaks. (Philippians 4:8, ESV)

Silence clarifies our purpose and calling and purifies our intentions and perceptions. Many of us are living lives based on lies from the Enemy or what culture shouts at us. For far too long, I confused self-denial with self-erasure and equated business with godliness. I was taking care of others and serving to the point that I was no longer caring well for myself. I had to confront what I thought a "good Christian woman" believes and looks like. When my health crashed, it changed to what does a person who "suffers well" believe and look like? I thought if salvation can't be earned, maybe healing can, and ended up bowing to the idol of self-sufficiency. I fell for the lies of "live what you feel" and "you deserve happiness" by believing culture gave me permission to blame God or others. But that only led me down a path of living as a perpetual victim of my circumstances. I wallowed between bitterness and apathetic resignation, grumbling about how unfair it is that others get to live so freely, and I'm constricted in where I can go, what I can eat, or how much I can handle in a day. I lived from a burden narrative, constantly feeling like I was "on the outside looking in," which made it feel easier to justify my pitiful existence.

What helped me to work through these lies was to start asking clarifying questions, aiming to uncover deep-seated thoughts, beliefs, and emotions. Who am I really, just like this, when no one is around? Why am I here? What am I doing with this life, and what is my motivation for pursuing that? What story am I telling myself or believing about this feeling or situation I'm dealing with? Where am I clamoring for attention? In my opinion, asking intentional questions isn't noisy because I'm seeking to dissect my beliefs and direct them to God. Much of the time, my internal noise is running amok in the background, so asking specific questions brings it to the foreground.

When I don't do this, I run the risk of letting false narratives cloud my vision and build up internally so that I end up living an incongruous life- one where my actions don't line up with my beliefs. Put another way, my walk doesn't match my talk.

Silence exposed my doubt, fear, insecurities, and anxieties. What we resist can persist, and what we focus on intensifies. So if I was focused on resisting symptoms or resisting a huge storm in my life, it only made sense that it felt overwhelming and all-consuming. When I was flat on my back, lying in bed or on the floor, I would cry out, lamenting my very existence, and when I felt emptied of words and tears, I let stillness and silence come. *Could I believe that I was seen, known, loved, and valued here and now, just like this? Or did I need my health or circumstances to change first? Am I loved and worthy even if I produce nothing?* When I couldn't run from my body or my thoughts, Jesus quieted me with His love and beckoned me to receive my true identity as His Beloved, which in turn had a direct impact on how I related to others.

Silence as Presence with Others

Silence has the potential to reveal what is going on beneath the surface of our lives. But that, my friend, is just the beginning. When we have the courage to surrender and attend to His presence, let Scripture read us and yield to the Holy Spirit's pruning, we get to be formed into people who reflect Jesus' love to the world around us.

I likely don't have to convince you of the value there is in practicing restraint with our tongues, as Proverbs is full of examples like this one: "Even fools are thought wise if they keep silent, and discerning if they hold their tongue" (Proverbs 17:28, NIV). And another, "The tongue has the power of life and death..." (Proverbs 18:21, NIV). Words matter. They carry weight; therefore, silence also has merit.

An example of this is in the book of Job. He is called a servant of God and a man of integrity and loses his wealth (flocks and herds), his children, and his health. When his three friends find out, they visit him and weep, tearing their robes. But Job 2:13 also tells us, "they sat with him on the ground seven days and seven nights, and *no one spoke a word to him*, for they saw that his suffering was very great." (ESV, emphasis added) They were able to be a ministering presence to him by sitting in silence, not saying anything. It was only after time wore on that they began questioning his character. There are times and places where words cease or fall short. May we resist the temptation to fill in spaces of silence with foolish words or made-up explanations that can often do more harm than good.

Silence is an affront to outrage commentary, defensive opinions, and the tyranny of excess noise. Whether online or in person, we can choose not to immediately participate in a debate or conversation. We don't have to get caught up in the web of sticky vitriol or contribute our voice unless we have taken a pause and believe that we will add value by speaking. Silence helps discipline us to exercise restraint and self-control out of respect for ourselves and others.

It is normal for silence to feel useless, inconvenient, or boring, because withdrawal from noise isn't supposed to feel completely painless. Trust the practice. Silence is cumulative and contributes to regulating our nervous systems, especially when combined with breathwork or breath prayers. This is how silence forms resilience in us so that we can show up and face whatever and whomever we encounter with an increased capacity for sustained attention. An indicator that this was working in my life was when going out to eat at busy restaurants with friends, I noticed that even being in close quarters with people surrounding our booth or table, I could easily focus on my friends, and the buzz of other conversations around me faded into white noise in the background.

If peace doesn't always mean the absence of chaos, then silence doesn't always mean the absence of noise (or sound). This isn't about rejecting all multi-tasking, rather reducing different kinds of noise to be faithful stewards of our bodies as hosts of the Holy One and attuning to His presence within. Noise accumulates in our souls the same way that excess stuff can clutter our homes. I usually know when I've reached my noise limit or threshold. Some personal indicators that I've noticed are being brusque or irritable with others, feeling extra anxious, hurried, overloaded, or exhausted, and wanting to isolate myself from the world. So what do I do about it? I practice slower, single-tasking, if possible. For example, when doing laundry or washing dishes, I will forgo listening to music or podcasts so I can better focus on the task at hand. I may sit or lie totally still and pray, confessing the lack of honor I have shown for my body or for my poor attitude and actions towards others. I rest in His presence. While driving longer distances, I challenge myself to see how long I can go without adding any additional noise. I simply converse with the Lord internally or aloud, voicing questions and listening. Wherever my mind wanders, I follow the trail, giving attention to matters that may be pressing on me by spending time processing with the Holy Spirit. Often, I focus on simple breathing exercises and breath prayers. I'll sing song lyrics that arise within. If people come to mind, I intercede for them, and before I know it, I'm arriving at my destination, usually feeling refreshed and peaceful. Here's a caveat, though: don't force resolution or answers to come. If you get stuck, you may need to call a friend or listen to music to interrupt the trap of overintrospection.

Remember, this isn't just about escaping noise, because that isn't always in our control, but rather cultivating presence wherever we are, even if that means listening to a children's chapter book being read aloud. I am pleased to say that I have grown tremendously in this area and believe there is mutual joy and gratitude being shared during my daughter's bedtime routine, as I can genuinely engage if she decides to ask me a question about the reading. When the distractions come, I gently tell myself *that the thought can wait until I leave her room.*

As followers of Jesus, we carry abundant life wherever we go and belovedness into every interaction. It is my prayer that you let silence invite you to behold the mystery and beauty of fellowship with our Triune God and that you discover how real treasure lies in cultivating a purity of silence in our souls, allowing us to remain secure in the Prince of Peace, even when the chaos of the world abounds. And in so doing, we become the kind of people who live out the greatest commandment: to love God with all of our heart, soul, mind, and strength and to love our neighbor as ourselves. (Mark 12:30-31, NIV).

Next Steps

Here are some ways that you can practically pursue more silence in your life:

1. Start with simply noticing the amount of noise in your daily life. Similar to keeping track of finances or protein intake- how much time are you spending in generally noisy environments, intentionally or unintentionally?

2. Try fasting from informational noise of content overload, whether news, social media, or Christian podcasts/videos/articles. Do this incrementally if needed. Take a day, week, or month off from your usual consumption routine.

3. Spend time with God in complete silence and focus on another sense. Instead of listening or watching something, listen for His voice. Listen to nature. Go

on a silent walk or hike. Try standing outside during a snowfall, especially at night. You could try focusing on tasting and savoring your food, looking outside, lighting a candle, or diffusing some essential oils. Delight in being present right in the moment you are in because life and breath come from Him. You may choose to add some instrumental music as purposeful sound, rather than background noise. Worship Him through praise, gratitude, and even lament.

4. Shut down whatever noise is in your control and get curious about your current thoughts and emotions. What's dominating your mental space? Can you name any feelings associated with that?

5. Invite a friend or small group to participate in any of this with you. You could practice one of these options together by setting a timer for an amount of your choosing and then taking turns sharing with each other how the time went by, building active listening skills.

6. For an extra challenge: attend a silent retreat near you or create your own. Start with 3 hours or half of a day and work up to a weekend or an entire week.

Final Note: If practicing silence for even five minutes is too triggering or overwhelming, that is okay. You may need to work through some of these with a safe person you trust, like a friend, therapist, spiritual director, or pastor. There is much grace for the journey.

*

About the
Authors

Vanessa King

Vanessa King is an emerging author who loves everything domestic. A hobbit at heart, her favorite place is at home with her books, garden, and loved ones. At home, she's likely homeschooling her kids, pursuing one of her many hobbies, and enjoying time with family and friends, with coffee in hand. When she's not at home, she's probably thrifting, hanging out with her best friend, or exploring somewhere new with her family. Above all, she's grateful for her loving and supportive husband, Micah, and for the love, care, and faithfulness of God throughout her life, which carry her through each day.

Website: www.pursuesimplejoy.com

Instagram: www.instagram.com/pursuesimplejoy/

www.instagram.com/theintentionalpen/

Facebook: www.facebook.com/pursuesimplejoy

Rosalene Luxem

osalene Luxem is a daughter of the King, living in the midst of the mundane and messy, determined to seek out God's goodness amid the reality of suffering. She lives in the beautiful Pacific Northwest with her son and their dog, Honey. In her free time, Rosalene can often be found playing board games with her son, snuggled under a blanket on the couch with a cup of tea, walking the paths of her favorite nearby beach with Honey, or laughing with her family and friends over small things that bring joy.

Substack: www.substack.com/@rosalenewrites

Instagram: www.instagram.com/rosalene.writes/

Lauren Ulrich

auren Ulrich lives in the Lowcountry of South Carolina, where she serves as a wife and homeschool mom to her three boys. She enjoys serving in her local church and is passionately committed to supporting pro-life activism and Biblical womanhood. She's witnessed God's miraculous power and faithfulness in her journey of growing up without a father. She's passionate about helping other women find security in the love of their Heavenly Father as an "Abba's girl." (Romans 8:15) She joyfully anticipates more opportunities to inspire women to stay anchored in the Father's love through speaking and writing.

Facebook: www.facebook.com/abbasgirlblog/

www.facebook.com/lulrich84/

Dawn Fowler

Dawn was born and raised in Chicago, Illinois, and lives there today with her family. She has been a passionate teacher for 26 years and discovered her love for reading and writing in college. She has written a book of poetry and has found joy in writing for Hope Books to share her faith. She is a strong believer that having faith in God can change and transform your life. She believes that her biggest accomplishments in life have been her relationship with God and helping others. She knows that teaching and writing have allowed her to do so, and she is very grateful to be able to share her experience with others.

Karen Bedells

Karen Hill Bedells is a Southern girl raised in the small town of Raymond, Mississippi. Along with her husband of 36 years, Barry, she lives in nearby Brandon. Karen is the proud mother of four daughters and is thankful for their four guys! She treasures time with her six grandchildren, whether on the ball field, in school plays, playing dress-up, or cooking. Called to nursing and missions over 40 years ago, she is a nurse practitioner who devotes her life to caring for others. In her writing, she desires to point others to Jesus, his faithfulness, and his peace in every season.

Instagram: www.instagram.com/queenb_karebear/

Facebook: www.facebook.com/KarenHillBedells

Linked In: www.linkedin.com/in/karen-hill-bedells-b61462117

Julie Baldwin

Julie Baldwin is a Pastor, Spiritual Director, companion on the journey of faith, and Nanna to three gorgeous girls. She holds a deep love for creating hospitable spaces where souls can breathe, and hearts can grow more deeply rooted in God's abiding love. Through *Welcome Soul*, Julie offers reflections and resources to help you live your faith with intention and grace.

Website: www.welcomesoul.com.au

Instagram: www.instagram.com/welcomesoulspace/

Facebook: www.facebook.com/profile.php?
id=61573717182809

Chere Wehling

Chere Wehling is a recovering worrier. She married her high school sweetheart, and her ambitious husband has provided ample opportunities for growth in her life, including learning to ride a motorcycle and snowmobile in less-than-ideal circumstances. She has two grown children and likes to joke; they raised her. When Chere isn't working as a cardiac nurse or teaching at her small church, she can be found at the piano or with a book in hand, or starting a baked treat in the kitchen. She is inspired by noticing God's lessons in everyday life.

Substack: www.substack.com/@cherewehling261965?

Instagram: www.instagram.com/wehlingc/

Facebook: www.facebook.com/chere.r.wehling

Becky Sims

Becky Sims has a strong faith in Jesus and a love for writing encouraging letters. She is the author of the *Porch Chair Prayers* devotional blog and book series. She prays that her writing will help other women longing to grow closer to the Lord to gain hope and meaning in their lives, while looking forward with confidence to eternity in heaven. Becky is a wife and mother, Hope*Writer, former teacher, and author. She is active in her church choir. She especially enjoys quiet time with the Lord and often spends time on her porch chair in prayer.

Website: www.porchchairprayers.com

www.porchchairprayers.com/newsletter

Instagram: www.instagram.com/beckysims22

Facebook: www.facebook.com/beckysims22

Alana Deutschmann

Alana Deutschmann is a native Minnesotan loving life in central Iowa with her daughter, Zahra. A contributor to the Year of Hope devotional book, she has a growing passion for Christian Spiritual Formation and encouraging others to live from their identity as God's Beloved. Alana currently works as a small town coffee shop manager, enjoys spending quality time with family and friends, and investing in her local church. Hobbies include reading, exercising, watching tennis, traveling, and listening to too many podcasts.

Substack: www.substack.com/@alanamaria22

Endnotes

Chapter 5

1. Hershey, Doug. "The True Meaning of Shalom // Defining Shalom — Firm Israel." *Fellowship of Israel Related Ministries*, 3 Jan. 2020, firmisrael.org/learn/the-meaning-of-shalom/.

2. Rothschild, Jennifer. *Psalm 23 The Shepherd Within Me*. Lifeway Press, 2018. Streaming on https://www.lifeway.com/en/product-family/psalm-23, 2022.

3. Hull, Eleanor H., versifier, and Mary E. Byrne, translator. *"Be Thou My Vision, O Lord of My Heart."* 8th Century, Irish Hymn. Please note there are many translations.

Chapter 7

1. Gluck, Jonathan. *An Exercise in Uncertainty*. Harmony Books. 2025. Kindle Edition

2. *Strong's #6960: qavah — Greek/Hebrew Definitions."* **Bible Tools**, https://www.bibletools.org/index.cfm/fuseaction/Lexicon.show/ID/H6960/qavah.htm. Accessed 21 Jan. 2026

3. Jethani, Skye. *With, Reimagining the Way You Relate to God*, Thomas Nelson, 2011

Chapter 8

1. Sleeth, Matthew, and Eugene H. Peterson. *24/6: A Prescription for a Healthier, Happier Life.* Tyndale House Publishers, 2012.

Chapter 9

1. Live Better Hearing, "Loud Movies & Noise-Induced Hearing Loss, 13 Dec 2022, www.livebetterhearing. com. Accessed Feb 22, 2026.

Closing

Dear Reader,

Thank you for reading *Peace:Resting in God in Every Storm!*

I want to take a moment to celebrate the incredible authors who contributed to this meaningful book. They have poured their hearts into discovering, clarifying, and sharing their unique messages—and now, you get to benefit from their hard work and dedication.

At hope*books, we are deeply proud of our authors and are honored to partner with them on this journey. If you've ever considered writing and publishing your book, we invite you to visit hopebooks.com to learn more about our coaching and publishing services. We believe that everyone has a message to share and an audience to serve, and the world needs your hopeful words now more than ever.

Once again, let's take a moment to celebrate the hard work of these authors in bringing *Peace:*

Resting in God in Every Storm to life.

Sincerely,

Brian Dixon

Publisher, hope*books

Looking to *connect* with a
community of writers?

www.hopewriters.com

The world needs your

hope-filled words

more now than ever before.

Thinking about *writing*
your own book?

www.hopebooks.com